LOVE KILLS

The quiet, fall Michigan evening was shattered by what Diane found inside her mailbox. On a single piece of paper someone had pasted together a sentence made of cutout letters from a magazine. The cryptic message simply read: *"You'll be sorry you didn't have lunch with me."*

Diane's normal control dissolved, and she began to shake and sob simultaneously. A horrendous feeling of panic swept over her. The letter confirmed what she had feared for weeks, that she was being stalked by an obsessed fan. It was likely he was still in the area. Or worse, inside her house.

Still clutching the letter, Diane quickly turned the Jeep around and sped back toward Cindy's house. When she arrived there, her sobs had turned into hysterics.

Diane shoved the letter into Cindy's hands. "They know where I live!" she screamed.

LOVE KILLS

THE STALKING OF DIANE NEWTON KING

ANDY HOFFMAN

AVON BOOKS ◆ NEW YORK

LOVE KILLS: THE STALKING OF DIANE NEWTON KING is
an original publication of Avon Books. This work has never before
appeared in book form. This work is a novel.

AVON BOOKS
A division of
The Hearst Corporation
1350 Avenue of the Americas
New York, New York 10019

First Avon Books Printing: July 1994

AVON TRADEMARK REG. U.S. PAT. OFF. AND IN OTHER COUNTRIES, MARCA
REGISTRADA, HECHO EN U.S.A.

Printed in the U.S.A.

RA   10   9   8   7   6   5   4   3   2   1

To my grandmother, Helen Schweitzer, who taught me at an early age that adversity is only one small step from achievement. Her support has been unending, her love undeniable.

ACKNOWLEDGMENTS

During the months that I have spent writing this book, I have become indebted to hundreds of people who gave their time and energy to this project. I am eternally grateful to all those who allowed me to intrude upon their lives.

Without question, the person most responsible for completing this book is my wife, Teresa. Her contribution to this book is immeasurable. She encouraged me when I needed it and berated me when I deserved it.

I also must thank Loralee Baker-Rapue whose tireless editing once again helped transform a series of interviews and newspaper articles into a book. It would not have been possible without her.

I would also like to thank Bob and Pat Hoffman, Roger and Shirley Johnson, Trace Christenson, Scott Smith, Randy Attwood, Herb Shuey, Mary Jo O'Brien and Randy Austin. Their assistance has been immense. I would also like to thank my agent, Carol Mann.

Finally, I wish to thank my editor at Avon Books, David Highfill. His patience and understanding has been overwhelming. His even-handed approach has made this journey extremely enjoyable. Thanks again, David.

CHAPTER 1

Oct. 30, 1990

It was Halloween Eve, and Diane Newton King had just completed her shift as the morning anchor at WUHQ-TV in Battle Creek, Michigan. The 34-year-old woman, now eight months pregnant, had become a popular local personality since moving from Colorado with her husband and young son.

In the two years that Diane had worked at WUHQ, she had developed a persona that transcended her celebrity status as a television anchor. Whether it was a local food drive, a Salvation Army fund-raiser or an effort to educate children about her Native American culture, Diane was always eager to help.

She was a career woman to some, a working mother to others, and a tireless volunteer to all. Not only did she have the energy, she usually provided the ideas.

"Someday I want people from coast to coast to know who Diane Newton is," she had often told family members as a child growing up in Sterling Heights, Michigan. "I want them to remember who I am and what I have accomplished in my life."

But on this day Diane was tired, irritable. It seemed her world was collapsing around her. After a routine day at work, she had picked up her 2-year-old son, Marler,

1

from day care, and driven to the home of a coworker to talk.

Cindy Accusta, a perky 33-year-old blonde, had become close friends with Diane since joining the television station several months before. She had trained under Diane and occasionally substituted for Diane as the morning anchor.

The one-hour visit with Cindy helped. Driving home, Diane was revitalized. Cindy was probably right, maybe it was the pregnancy that had made her money and marriage problems seem so enormous. She promised herself her life would be better after the baby was born. She glanced in her rearview mirror at Marler strapped in his car seat. His playful, innocent smile made her feel less anxious.

She turned her Jeep Wagoneer west onto Division Drive and into the setting sun. Diane and her husband, Brad, had moved from their townhouse in Battle Creek to a farm just outside Marshall, a historic town of 7,500 people a few miles southeast of Battle Creek in south central Michigan.

Diane loved Marshall and its quaint, small-town business district lined with antique shops and mom-and-pop restaurants. She had only lived there a few months, but she felt at home. Because of her television exposure, she was a celebrity in the town and had been quickly adopted by the close-knit community.

Diane drove slowly down the tree-lined lane toward the isolated farmhouse she and Brad had rented just outside the city limits. Diane loved the two-story white-frame house, even though it needed remodeling and Brad had been slow in accomplishing what he had promised when they moved in. Regardless, she cherished the long walks they took on the property and dreamed of raising their children there.

Pulling into the driveway, she knew Brad would not be home. As a part-time criminology instructor at Western Michigan University in Kalamazoo, about 30 minutes away, Brad was teaching classes on Tuesday and Thursday evenings that semester. He normally left home about midday and didn't return until late evening.

Diane stopped at the mailbox that was on a post near the edge of the road. The quiet, fall Michigan evening was shattered by what Diane found inside the mailbox. On a single piece of paper, someone had pasted together a sentence made of cutout letters from a magazine. The cryptic message simply read: "You'll be sorry you didn't have lunch with me."

Diane's usual control dissolved, and she began to shake and sob simultaneously. She felt the baby lurch inside her. She didn't know what to do. A horrendous feeling of panic swept over her. She turned toward Marler, then back toward the house that sat about 50 yards from the road. Her eyes scanned the house, the barn and the other outbuildings nearby. Nothing seemed disturbed. Everything was serene.

Diane suppressed the sobs in an effort not to frighten Marler. It didn't work. She couldn't control her emotions. The letter confirmed what Diane had feared for weeks—that she was being stalked by an obsessed fan. And if that was true, it was likely he was still in the area, or worse, inside her house.

Still clutching the letter, Diane quickly turned the Jeep around and sped back toward Cindy's house. When she arrived, her sobs had turned into hysterics.

"They know where I live," she screamed, shoving the letter into Cindy's hands. "I just found this in my mailbox."

As a coworker, Cindy was fully aware of the harassing telephone calls Diane had received at work during the past few months. Initially, the calls seemed to be from someone interested in learning about the television business. The caller, who asked a series of questions, always asked Diane to lunch. At first the calls were a nuisance, part of being in the public eye. But when they continued despite her emphatic rejections, Diane became frustrated. During one call she told the person off and slammed down the telephone. It was a moment of anger she regretted.

Larry Nienhaus, Diane's supervisor at WUHQ-TV, had taken one of the telephone calls for her. He later told investigators that the caller had talked with a muffled voice and that it was obvious the man was attempting to conceal his true identity. He said the caller appeared "not to have it all together, not a clear-thinking, rational person, but a kook."

The late 1980s had seen a dramatic rise in the stalking of movie stars, celebrities, television reporters and others in the public eye. Several high-profile cases had been documented in the media, and Diane was acutely aware of the growing problem people in her profession faced. She asked the station to help implement safety procedures, including screening all her telephone calls.

Diane also got an unlisted telephone number and had Brad remove their names from the mailbox in front of their house.

Now, Cindy and her husband, Juan, helped the frightened Diane inside. Cindy called the Calhoun County Sheriff's Department and requested that an officer come to their house.

Diane also called Brad at Western Michigan and left a message for him.

When Officer Albert Lemkuhl arrived at the Accustas' house shortly before 6 P.M., he put gloves on and gently placed the letter into a plastic envelope to maintain any fingerprints that might be on the letter. Although Diane, Cindy and Juan had handled it, the fingerprints of the person who had sent the letter possibly could be identified.

After a brief discussion with Lemkuhl about the letter

and the recent telephone calls at work, Diane hesitantly agreed to return to her farmhouse with the officer to investigate any possible break-in. Diane left Marler with the Accustas, making it clear that she would return with the officer and wouldn't go home again until Brad returned from Western Michigan later that night.

A thorough search of the premises revealed nothing unusual. There seemed to have been no attempt to get inside the house, and there was no indication in the barn or the other outbuildings that anything had been disturbed. Regardless, Diane was petrified that someone knew where she lived and what she was doing.

"Whoever it is must be following me," she tearfully told Lemkuhl.

Diane and the officer returned to the Accustas' house where she waited for Brad. She had been upset with Brad over his lack of concern about the telephone calls, and now her anger was growing with every minute that passed without him coming to her aid.

Brad had been a police officer for 12 years in Pontiac, Michigan, and Diane wanted to believe that his indifference was based on his years of experience investigating threats that never materialized. But she also felt that as her husband he should be more understanding and compassionate.

Brad did arrive about 10 P.M., but once again showed little concern.

"Diane's downstairs if you want to be alone with her," Cindy told him, well aware of Diane's building anger. "She's waiting for you."

Instead of going downstairs, Brad nonchalantly began picking up Marler's toys and clothes.

Cindy became tense and uncomfortable. The contrasts were obvious. Diane was visibly upset about the letter, but Brad seemed uninterested, indifferent to Diane's feelings.

"All he wanted to do was leave," Cindy later recalled.

While Diane had waited for Brad to return, she discussed with Cindy and Juan what precautions they should take. Outside security lights, new locks and a guard dog were each possible options.

When Brad was told of their talk, he responded dispassionately.

"I want to see what the station's going to do about this first. Are you ready to go home, Diane?" he said, ending the conversation abruptly.

At home, an argument started. Diane was adamant that security precautions be taken.

"I don't know why you are so worried about this," Brad said, disgustedly. "Nothing is going to happen to you. You don't have to worry about this. You're overreacting."

Diane's fears did not subside. In fact, they increased. Whether or not Brad believed she was in danger really didn't matter to Diane. The fact was, she believed the threats were real, and, true to her nature, decided to take matters into her own hands.

Within a few days, she had instituted a plan she hoped would ensure her safety. The Calhoun County Sheriff's Department, at Diane's insistence, began regular patrols in the area. Deputies also promised to try to find the source of the threatening letter, telling Diane they would ask Michigan's state crime lab to identify the fingerprints on the document. Officials at WUHQ made everyone at the station aware of the letter and its possible implications for Diane's security.

After several heated arguments, even Brad acquiesced to Diane's demands. New locks were installed, and floodlights were erected around the farmhouse. And despite Brad's protests that he was allergic to dogs, Diane got a Doberman pinscher from her sister, Darlene. Diane wanted the dog to stay in the house, or at least on the enclosed porch. But Brad said no. His allergies prohibited that. The dog was kept outside on a chain.

Diane also refused to return home alone if Brad was not there. Instead, she would enlist coworkers, friends or neighbors to accompany her. Before entering the house, Diane would circle the farmhouse in her Jeep Wagoneer, searching the doors and windows for signs of a break-in.

If Brad was scheduled to be at home, Diane would call from work to make sure he would be there when she arrived. Diane would pull into the driveway, honk the horn and wait for him to appear on the porch. Then, and only then, would she get out of the Jeep and go into the house.

Everyone who knew Diane was aware of her terror. A few weeks after receiving the threatening letter, Diane raced into the daycare center in Battle Creek where Marler stayed during the day. She was petrified that two men had followed her from work.

"She was really worried, afraid," recalled Elizabeth Way, a daycare worker. "She called the police because she wasn't sure who they were or what they wanted. She was definitely concerned about her safety and her child's safety."

A Battle Creek police officer came to the daycare center, but the officer was unable to identify who the men in the car were, whether they were actually following Diane or whether she was simply skittish about the letter and phone calls.

"She hoped it was some teenagers playing games," Way later said, "but because of the threatening letters she said she couldn't take a chance. She had to call the police."

Diane's life became one of constant suspicion and surveillance. Her fears began to affect her pregnancy. Two weeks before the scheduled birth of her daughter by cesarean section, Diane visited the small, quiet Oaklawn

Hospital in Marshall to review security measures there. At Diane's request, extra security was added, she was given a private room and her visitors were limited to immediate family and a few close friends.

"I don't want anyone to know I am here," she emphatically told hospital employees. "No one."

CHAPTER 2

DIANE AND BRAD were an unlikely pair. Almost 10 years apart in age, they were from different ethnic and social backgrounds. Brad had grown up in a family of bankers. Diane's family had struggled as blue-collar workers.

Although opposites in almost every way, they had one thing in common: a lifelong quest to improve themselves. It was not surprising that they had met in the early 1980s at an EST seminar—a self-improvement program founded by Werner Erhard to create inner peace through self-exploration and self-deprivation. They were introduced by Brad's college fraternity brother, Randy Wright, also an EST disciple.

Brad had migrated to Erhard's rigid, demanding training while a member of the Pontiac police department. He liked the introspection that EST encouraged. So did Diane.

When Brad and Diane met, Diane was finishing her bachelor's degree in communications at Wayne State University and awaiting her commission in the United States Army. Brad, a 13-year police veteran with a master's degree in criminal justice, was planning to leave the police department to work full time for the EST group.

Although both had college degrees, they had achieved their educational goals through distinctly different paths.

Brad had relied on his parents to fund his education. Diane had worked her way through college with part-time jobs. She joined the ROTC to help defray her education costs. She was determined to become a broadcast journalist.

Born in April 1956 in Detroit, Diane was one of five children. Her mother, Freida, was a full-blooded Mohawk whose relatives still lived on a reservation in Canada.

When Diane was 9 years old, her father died. She would never get over his death. With each year that passed, her memories of him grew.

"Diane put her dad on a pedestal," said one childhood friend. "She put him up there with the Kennedys. He wasn't only her father, he was her idol."

While growing up, Diane shunned her Native American heritage. She tried hard to be an "average American" child. Always afraid she was overweight and unattractive, she did whatever she could to fit in. She became an overachiever. While others around her struggled to survive, Diane dreamed of a successful future, full of glamour and excitement.

"She loved the royalty in England," said another friend. "She liked to dream of their fantasy life. Diane was a real go-getter. She felt her sisters had settled for something less than they could have in terms of their lives and careers. Diane was determined not to let that happen to her."

Diane also developed traits as a young woman that would enhance her career but, eventually, damage her private life. She was quick to judge and even quicker to condemn. Her tongue was her weapon, and it could be devastating.

"She did not have a wide range of friends due to her very strong personality," said Carlo Lonnie Eaton, a close friend of Diane's in the late 1970s and early 1980s. "Diane was not a woman whom a lot of women would like. She was always dressed immaculately. She had a lot of self-esteem. It was very important to Diane that people be honest with her and to say what was on their minds. Diane did not like people who would wimp out or back down."

Diane also strived hard to be the best and look the best.

"She was a yuppie long before there were yuppies," another friend recalled.

When Diane first met Brad, he seemed to be the perfect mate. Like her, he was determined to improve himself. He was well-educated, articulate and Anglo, an extremely important detail to Diane at that stage of her life. She thought it would be easier to break the barriers of racism with an "Anglo" husband.

"Diane looked upon Brad as someone she could count on," an acquaintance of the couple later recalled. "She thought he was honest and straightforward. She wasn't concerned that he had been married before. Based on what Brad had told her, she didn't think the divorce was his fault."

While Diane had been independent and self-motivated her entire life, Brad had been a mama's boy. He was a loner. Members of the Pontiac police force described him as "introverted to the point of arrogance."

Brad, the older of two sons, was born in 1947 to Willis and Marjorie Lundeen. Brad had spent an uneventful childhood growing up in Croswell, Michigan, where his father was president of a bank.

"Brad wasn't close to anyone, really," his mother recalled. "He was somewhat of a loner most of his life. Although he had friends, he never had a best friend."

It was not until he joined the Tau Kappa Epsilon fraternity at Western Michigan University in Kalamazoo that he seemed to emerge from the shadows. He showed talents as an organizer and communicator. He represented his fraternity on several boards and committees, and he was elected the TKE's man of the year. He felt comfortable working within the fraternity framework.

"He seemed happy," said a friend and fraternity brother. "He really enjoyed being a TKE."

While in college, Brad met and married his first wife, Gail Heitzker.

Brad's goals of becoming a third-generation banker faded during his junior year of college. He longed to be a teacher, but eventually gravitated toward police work. He liked the power, authority and respect that came with the badge.

He joined the Pontiac Police Department shortly after graduation. During his nearly 13 years with the department, he spent a large part of his time as a liaison officer at Pontiac Central High School, working as a counselor and confidante to students. He enjoyed police administration rather than patrol work or criminal investigations. He also worked part-time as an instructor at Henry Ford Community College.

While at the Pontiac Police Department, he assisted superiors in investigating minor cases of corruption against two of his partners. However, his involvement in the investigation was more a result of circumstance than duty.

Regardless of his involvement in the corruption cases, many officers within the department disliked him.

"Brad thought he was an intellectual, above everyone else," said one police officer who worked with him. "He was a reserved person who wasn't easy to get along with. He was a loner and always tried to impress people. He was always the odd man out. Brad wasn't close to anyone."

Another officer remembered Brad as a "strange duck who was lazy and never did his share of the work. He always seemed to be preoccupied with matters that didn't relate to his job as a police officer."

He also had a reputation within the police department as a womanizer, a perception he did nothing to change.

The first few years of Brad's 13-year marriage to Gail were happy. They were financially independent, partly because he maintained full-time employment. But more important, they were happy because Gail made the major decisions. If Brad was having affairs, Gail wasn't aware of them. It wasn't until the birth of their daughter, Alissa, that their troubles began.

Brad was furious that Gail had become pregnant. Doctors had said that it would be medically impossible for her to have a child. Then, unexpectedly, she discovered the doctors were wrong. Brad was livid. He moved out of the house for six weeks, only to return after the baby was born. That was in 1972.

Almost 10 years after the birth of their daughter, Brad walked into their house and announced to Gail that he wanted a divorce. It didn't shock her.

"He wasn't satisfied with his role as husband and father," Gail later recalled. "I felt he just wanted to be on his own. I agreed."

The divorce was final in January 1982. A few months later, Brad met Diane. Initially, Diane and Brad's relationship also was rocky. Shortly after their meeting, Brad quit the police department and began working full-time for the EST organization. Brad moved to Cincinnati and eventually moved to Denver to continue working for the EST group.

Diane, recently discharged from the military, followed him to Colorado.

"At first, it seemed like they were constantly butting heads," a friend in Denver recalled of the months prior to their marriage. "They argued a lot and Diane decided she had had enough. She returned to Michigan."

What Diane didn't know was that during that separation, Brad also returned to Michigan. But he had another woman on his mind: Gail. He arrived unannounced at his ex-wife's house and begged her to take him back. She rejected his marriage proposal, giving it little consideration. She was building a new life for herself and had no desire to remarry him.

"He had changed," she recalled. "He seemed a lot less mature than he did during our marriage. And I had a new life."

A few weeks later, still stung by Gail's rejection, Brad married Diane. The couple were wed in July 1984 in Denver. Freida, Diane's mother, acted as a witness.

Although Freida participated in her daughter's wedding, she was not pleased with her daughter's choice of a husband. For one thing, Brad was unemployed. He had left the EST group, disillusioned. His unemployment was an open wound that would fester for years.

"She could have done much better," Freida told relatives and friends upon her return from Denver.

Despite Freida's misgivings, the marriage seemed to be working, even if Brad wasn't. While Diane's career blossomed in Colorado, Brad's wilted. The once confident police officer found himself wandering aimlessly from job to job. Money was always short, but promises of new and better jobs were always on the horizon.

Diane, on the other hand, seemed to be on a career path to stardom. In Denver, Diane worked as a production research assistant and reporter for a public television station, KRMA-TV. She was well-respected, not only for her journalistic skills, but for her commitment to the community. She became active in volunteer work, sharing her time and energy with anyone who asked.

"Diane was caring, almost to the point of showing off," said Regina Zapinski, a friend. "But she wasn't showing off, that was just her personality. She always wanted to help."

Diane also began to rediscover her Native American heritage. During her youth in Michigan, the family's heritage had not been dramatically important to them. They visited relatives who still lived on the Canadian reservation and occasionally attended tribal functions, but it wasn't until Diane moved to Colorado that she embraced her family's background. Brad, who had been infatuated with Indians as a child, encouraged her.

While Diane was expanding her horizons, Brad was drifting. He worked as a counselor, private investigator, security consultant and at other jobs that seemed to have little or no future.

In 1987, after almost two-and-a-half years at the public television station, Diane was hired as general assignment reporter at KJCT-TV in Grand Junction, Colorado. Brad followed her and, for the first time, seemed to accept the fact that Diane's career was the number one priority in their marriage. It was something friends and coworkers noticed almost immediately.

"I think Brad liked being Mr. Diane King," one friend later said. "But there was something in the relationship for Diane, too. I think she liked being the one in charge."

Others who knew them believed the couple to be complete opposites.

"Diane was a very aggressive reporter," said coworker Jacqueline Pyle. "She was very active in the community. Brad had absolutely no motivation. It seemed he was happy just to tag along with Diane and see what happened with her career."

And in charge she was. Like Gail had done in his first marriage, Diane handled the financial matters and made most of the important decisions.

"Diane loved him dearly, but she was becoming increasingly upset that he couldn't keep a job," said Teresa Nisley, a friend. "She couldn't understand why."

Despite ongoing family problems, Diane continued to maintain outwardly that everything was perfect. The community activism she had started in Denver grew in Grand Junction. She became involved in several community and charitable organizations, including Partners, a non-profit group that teamed adult role models with troubled youths.

Brad participated in the Partners program with Diane and dutifully attended most of the functions. However, he always remained in the background, content as an observer.

Diane also was making a name for herself in journalism. Her community affairs program, "News 8 Forum," was selected by the Colorado Broadcasters Association for excellence in journalism.

"I never got a reporter so involved in the community," her boss, Mike Moran, told reporters shortly after her death. "I usually have to push my reporters. She was definitely the most aggressive reporter I have ever had."

In the midst of her professional success, Diane became pregnant with her first child. Initially, Brad was again angry about a pregnancy. But eventually he accepted it. Marler, named after Diane's father, was born in March 1988.

Despite Diane's success, financial problems were beginning to weigh heavily. In addition to their own bills, Brad's inability to find and keep a permanent job was preventing him from paying his child support payments to Gail.

The financial problems, combined with Brad's difficulty in getting along with his daughter, Alissa, strained relationships between Brad's two families: his ex-wife and daughter, and Diane.

Once again Brad sat in the background as Diane and his ex-wife, Gail, took center stage. Diane didn't like the way Alissa treated her father, and Gail didn't like the way Diane treated Alissa. After several heated exchanges over the treatment of her daughter, Gail wrote a letter to Brad and Diane that illustrated the dominance the women had in his life. The letter was searing.

"Brad, I am aware that you have attempted to communicate with Alissa for several years," Gail wrote. "If she chooses not to risk her feelings again and open up to you, she must accept the consequences. Possibly, you two can settle your differences at a later date.

"In the interim, if you continue to allow your self-appointed mouthpiece (Diane) the opportunity to destroy every relationship you should be striving to maintain, you'll have many regrets. I will not subject Alissa to this constant emotional browbeating. If individuals, even children, receive love, respect and fairness on an ongoing basis, they reciprocate with similar behavior . . .

"Diane, everyone cannot be out-of-step but you. Your immature outbursts do not air opinions, instead they insult and hurt feelings. These continuous confrontations with inaccurate statements convince me that you truly are a rude, arrogant, insensitive and ignorant person. If your child is half as successful as mine at 15 years, I'll be amazed. Your parenting skills are zero and your common sense is non-existent. Do not ever oblige yourself to communicate with me again.

"Brad, a lawyer will be contacting you to settle our financial agreements. This is my last communique with either of you. Any contact with Alissa will strictly be up to her. I'm not known for flexibility or patience, but you both have my deepest sympathy."

When the letter arrived, Diane was furious, Brad humiliated and Gail pleased. Within a few weeks, the financial problems were resolved. To satisfy his child support responsibilities, Brad gave Gail his share of the equity in the house they had bought together years before.

Although he was relieved of the financial burden of child support payments, he and Diane still struggled to meet monthly bills. Then the third woman in Brad's life re-entered the picture: his mother. Whenever Brad would find himself struggling, he would telephone his mother for assistance.

Although Brad rarely saw her, Marjorie Lundeen continued to play an important role in his life. She was the safety net he and Diane used repeatedly.

"I usually gave Brad small amounts," his mother said later. "The requests would run around $1,000 at a time. It was usually to pay bills."

In addition to money problems, Brad and Diane were facing another, more personal, problem. Marler's birth threatened Brad. Freida remembered visiting Brad and Diane in Grand Junction after Marler's birth. Diane was ecstatic, Brad was moody and jealous of Marler. He drifted into self-pity.

"He felt neglected," Freida recalled. "He didn't think he was getting to spend enough time with Diane."

But with time, Brad seemed to accept Marler, and even began to like his role as a "Mr. Mom." He prided himself on being able to take care of his son.

"It gave him something to be proud of," a friend in Grand Junction said.

Within months of Marler's birth, Diane began longing to go home to her family. She dreamed of returning to Michigan where she could be close to her parents. Because of Brad's inability to keep a job in Colorado, he too wanted to move back to Michigan. He dreamed of completing his doctoral degree—a goal he had dreamed of for years.

Diane started sending resumes to television stations in Michigan. Eleven months after Marler's birth, Diane was hired to work for WUHQ-TV in Battle Creek. She would be the morning anchor, doing five-minute break-ins during "Good Morning America."

Brad also found employment. He was hired by the Calhoun County Mental Health Department in Battle Creek. Brad, Diane and Marler moved into a townhouse in Battle Creek.

Initially, the move seemed to work. Diane liked her job as the morning anchor at WUHQ. She was given opportunities to produce documentaries—one of which won the Michigan Education Association School Bell award. They seemed happy. Brad even found a better job. In October 1989, Brad was hired as a probation officer for the Calhoun County District Court.

Diane also continued her community work, serving on the Salvation Army board of directors and working for the United Arts Council and the Michigan Food Bank. She joined the Junior Service League. She also became deeply involved in the Indian community in Michigan, regularly attending powwows.

She began to pursue a plan to develop curriculum for elementary school children that would educate them about the real life of Native Americans, not the Hollywood version that she had grown up with.

She seemed fulfilled. For the first time in a long time, Brad too seemed satisfied.

Unfortunately, the satisfaction was short-lived. Within three months of being hired, Brad was fired as a probation officer, accused by court officials of falsely filling out his time card to reflect more hours than he had actually worked.

Diane was angry and embarrassed; she demanded an explanation. Brad denied any wrongdoing. As he had always done in the past, he looked for someone else to blame. He accused district court personnel of harboring a grudge against him. He told Diane he would file a lawsuit that would eventually exonerate him.

The move back to Michigan, designed to bring Diane closer to her family and to allow Brad to work on his doctoral degree, exploded in Diane's face. Once again, the bills started to mount. The Internal Revenue Service filled a lien on her wages at the station for back taxes. She blamed Brad for failing to fill out the tax forms correctly.

As a public figure, Diane relied on her reputation. Now it seemed she had been embarrassed by her own husband's actions.

She began to question the move. The financial problems they had sought to escape in Colorado were again part of their lives. Brad never did get along with her parents, and the move back to Michigan had increased the friction between Brad and Freida. She was a hard woman to please, and Brad had made little effort to do so. Brad could do nothing right in Freida's eyes, and he felt the same about her.

Again Brad couldn't find full-time employment. For eight months he did not work, Diane was solely responsible for providing financial support.

The only job Brad could find was as a part-time instructor at Western Michigan University. The pay was minimal and the chance to become a full-time professor was almost non-existent. It was a job, but it offered little hope for the future.

History was repeating itself. Brad drifted into depression. Once again, he found himself in Diane's shadow, unable to assert himself.

Although his appearance was intimidating, when he was around Diane he looked like a beaten man. He was humbled by his inability to maintain a job.

"Diane was always in control of every situation," remembered Kristina Mony, who worked with Diane at the television station. "I thought Diane was very intimidating to Brad. Her strength and independence suffocated his personality. Around her, he was very shy. A puppy dog."

CHAPTER 3

Fall 1990

TO THE PUBLIC, Diane's world seemed idyllic: She was a beautiful woman with a promising career and a wonderful family. To close friends and coworkers, it was a different story.

Diane was increasingly unhappy. To add to the growing financial burden, she was worried about losing her job. Rumors were circulating that the station might be sold. As the family's chief moneymaker, she couldn't afford to be out of work.

But most important, Diane was concerned about her marriage. Although she and Brad had had their financial difficulties in the past, the couple had been able to work through it. But things were changing. Brad seemed distant, preoccupied.

A marriage that had worked in spite of many problems for six years now seemed to be spiraling downward into chaos. It seemed to Diane that Brad had grown tired of the battles. In the fall of 1990, Brad seemed to be losing interest. Accustomed to being in charge, Diane now felt she was losing control. She and Brad seemed to argue about anything and everything.

Many of her friends attributed Diane and Brad's recent marital problems to her second pregnancy. They thought

21

Diane's mood swings were also due to a natural depression that sometimes accompanies a birth. But Diane knew it was more and admitted to family and friends that Brad was attending counseling.

"We don't want a divorce," she told a friend. "We really want this to work out. He's not a bad person. He's just had some tough times."

While she defended Brad to her parents and family, she chastised him privately. She accused him of being lazy, irresponsible and of not loving his son. Like her mother's, Diane's tongue could be sharp.

Once again Brad found himself in a relationship that was completely dominated by a woman. First it was his mother. Then it was Gail. Now it was Diane.

Brad felt alone, insecure and most of all angry at himself for not being able to control his own destiny. After one heated argument, again over his inability to keep a job, Brad wrote Diane a letter outlining his frustrations.

"Sometimes I get myself into a position and everything I do just gets worse," he wrote Diane. "I know that sometimes I don't demonstrate much commitment. But I assure you I am committed to us. If I weren't, I'd leave. And I am not leaving.

"Sometimes I wonder why I go through what I do and surely the easy answer is to give up. But when I think of you and my son I have all the reasons in the world to keep working it out. I love you both very much. I know that we are committed to the same basic values and purpose in life. I wouldn't want to do it with anyone else, that's for sure.

"I guess the saying is sometimes true that you hurt the ones you love the most. I know I don't communicate the way you do. I work hard at that and sometimes I fall short.

"I don't want you to think I don't have feelings for you because I do. I just get stuck and cannot get unstuck for awhile.

"Sometimes, especially lately, it seems to me I say things and you either misunderstand or aren't listening to me. I know you have a lot on your mind; with your job not being exactly what you want, your problems with the powers that be at WUHQ and even me, when I'm a big jerk.

"Please forgive me for leaving you with the impression that I was being insensitive to your needs given you don't feel good. I love you very much and am very committed to our relationship, even when it doesn't look like I am. Love, Brad."

Although normally hesitant to discuss her private life, Diane had recently confided to close friends that Brad had lost interest in her sexually.

"He told me I had bad hygiene and that I was dirty," Diane confided to a friend.

A few days before the baby was born, Brad and Diane got into an argument that escalated to the point of physical attack: Brad angrily struck Diane in the stomach. She was startled by his anger—he had never struck her before—and afraid that he might have injured their unborn child.

Brad, too, was startled by his own inability to control his emotions. He had spent his entire life concealing his feelings. The next morning when Diane awoke, she found a handwritten letter from Brad.

"Diane, I don't like being out of control any more than you do," he wrote in red ink on a yellow legal pad. "I'm not trying to be one up or better or anything like that. I'm just having a tough time communicating right now. I feel very bad that things got out of hand. Maybe I'm trying too hard to be your husband. I really want to be perfect."

The letter was typical of Brad: apologetic and remorseful.

"I love you and will use that to drive my awareness. We make mistakes. I don't think you are bad or dirty or anything. That isn't how we really want it to be. Talk to you in the morning. I love you very much."

On the day their daughter Kateri was born, Brad was by Diane's side. But he immediately left the hospital after the birth and didn't return until the next day. In part, he left because he had to teach a class that evening at Western Michigan University. But he stayed away primarily because Freida was in town for the birth of her granddaughter.

"She's a bitch," he told friends at the university. "Why would I want to spend any more time than I have to with her?"

Freida had returned to the farmhouse to watch Marler, but Brad remained at the university until early the next morning. Barb Elgutta, a close friend of Diane's, spent the evening at the hospital with Diane.

Although Diane was excited about the birth of her daughter, Barb thought Diane was consumed by anxiety.

"She seemed depressed, very sad," Barb said. "She was extremely happy about the birth of Kateri, but she was depressed about how her life was going."

Diane didn't want Barb to leave and, despite announcements that visiting time had expired, Barb stayed until almost 10 P.M.

"She just didn't want to be left alone," Barb said later. "She begged me to stay."

Kateri's birth didn't provide the stimulus Diane hoped would propel her and Brad back into the happiness they had known earlier in their marriage. In fact, the relationship continued to deteriorate.

"I could walk out of this marriage right now and never look back," Diane told a friend a few weeks after Kateri's birth. "I've had it with him."

Instead, they both agreed to work on their problems. They began to attend marriage counseling sessions together. Diane promised to be less demanding, and

Brad agreed to look for full-time employment.

Diane also started working diligently on her project to educate elementary school children on Native American heritage. She had approached the Kellogg Foundation about a $16,000 grant to fund the project.

She also started talking more earnestly about quitting her job at the television station in June to spend more time with her children and to work on the elementary school project. In spite of her promises during counseling, Diane continued to badger Brad about finding full-time employment, no matter what kind of job it was. It was a suggestion that Brad thought unacceptable. How would he continue to work on his doctoral degree if he had to get a full-time job?

Following Kateri's birth, Diane returned to Sterling Heights to visit family and friends. On maternity leave until the first of the year, Diane found solace in being around her family.

Because Diane and Brad had lived in Colorado when Marler was born, Freida had never spent much time with her grandson. Now that they were only a couple of hours away, it seemed natural for Diane to want to take the children to her mother's house as often as possible.

The trips were never more than two or three days, but Brad rarely accompanied them.

It was during one visit in early December that another incident occurred, one that upset Diane and left family members worried about her safety.

Diane had taken the children to Sterling Heights on Dec. 10 and had planned to spend a few days with her family and then return for WUHQ-TV's annual Christmas party.

On Dec. 11, Diane attempted to reach Brad at the farm in Marshall all day. When she couldn't, she left a message on their answering machine about 11:15 P.M., saying she had called.

Brad telephoned the next morning with bad news: Someone had tried to break into their house the night before. Brad told Diane that he had gotten home late from the university and gone directly to bed. A few hours later, he was awakened by the sound of footsteps on the back porch.

"I got up, loaded my shotgun, went out and got the dog and spent the rest of the night patroling the property," he told her. "I think you should stay at your mother's another night till we find out what is going on."

It had been one of her worst fears, the thought of someone breaking into her home and waiting for her to arrive. Diane was extremely upset. She questioned Brad about every aspect of the incident. He told her he had found pry marks on a porch door that indicated to him someone had attempted to enter the house. He told her he had already notified the Calhoun County Sheriff's Department, and they had been to the farmhouse and taken down a report.

"I just don't think it would be safe for you to be here right now," he said. "Stay a couple more days and I'll let you know if anything happens."

She hesitantly agreed. But she was puzzled by Brad's newfound interest in her safety. He had downplayed the telephone calls and threatening letters, but now seemed genuinely concerned that someone may have attempted to break into their home. She wondered why.

Diane returned to Marshall for the Christmas party. It was there that friends and coworkers realized the problems between Diane and Brad were increasing. What once had been strictly private now was becoming apparent to everyone. Fiercely proud, Diane had rarely let anyone know about problems between her and Brad.

At the WUHQ Christmas party, Diane and her friend Virginia Colvin had an unusual conversation about Brad's difficulties with Diane's family. Diane told Virginia that she didn't know what to do. She loved

Brad, but she also loved her mother. At one point, Diane told Virginia that she had confronted Freida about her disapproval of Brad.

"I just told her that the marriage isn't everything that I'd hoped it would be, but it is what it is and you have to accept it," Diane said.

Surprisingly, Brad was sitting at the same table during Diane and Virginia's discussion.

"Brad was sitting right there and heard every word of it," Virginia later recalled. "I was surprised by the fact that . . . Diane did all the talking. I wondered how he felt being in her shadow all the time. She basically ran the show. She was the star. He really didn't work. I wondered what it did to his self-esteem."

Privately, Brad seemed to find satisfaction in knowing that Diane had stood up to Freida. As a peace offering, Brad gave Diane a beautiful diamond ring for Christmas. She questioned how he could afford it. Brad shrugged it off, saying he had been putting small amounts of money away for months.

Diane, wanting the marriage to work, not only for herself, but to prove her mother wrong, was extremely happy. She didn't care where or how Brad had acquired the money to buy the ring, she was simply pleased that he had made the effort.

Throughout the holidays, the marriage seemed to improve. Away from the university atmosphere, Brad seemed to mellow. The couple spent more time together. They made plans to have Kateri baptized in early February at St. Mary's Catholic Church in Marshall. Diane's dream was to combine the traditional Catholic baptism with a ceremony reflecting her Indian heritage. It was going to be a unique, beautiful ceremony, she told friends and relatives.

Sister Josephine Karras assisted Diane and Brad in making plans for the baptism. She saw the couple on Feb. 4, 1991.

"At St. Mary's, we have the parents change the garments of the baby after the baptism to show the significance of the new life, of the cleansing that has just taken place," Sister Karras later explained. "The parents usually put white garments on the baby. Diane and Brad decided to put a white deerskin on the baby and put her first set of moccasins on her. Diane was also going to put a white rabbit fur on the baby to show cleanliness and the purity of the baby at that time.

"They seemed to be happy and proud of their new baby."

CHAPTER 4

Feb. 9, 1991

THE RADIO DISPATCHER'S urgent voice caught Deputy Guy Picketts' ear as he loaded equipment into his patrol car at his home in Marshall.

"It's a call for unknown trouble with injuries at 16240 Division Drive," the sheriff's dispatcher said as he ordered Deputy William Lindsay to respond.

Picketts knew the address well. It had been his home for several years. As he continued to monitor the radio traffic, he realized that Lindsay was several minutes away in Battle Creek.

"I'm close by, I'll respond," Picketts radioed the dispatcher as he backed his patrol car out of his driveway, turned onto Mansion Street and then headed south on US-27 toward the farmhouse just outside the Marshall city limits.

Picketts had moved with his family to the Marshall farmhouse when he was 16 years old and, except for a four-year stint in the Navy, he had lived there until the late 1970s. He loved the area, especially the solitude. He remembered the quiet fishing holes and the 500-acre sanctuary behind the house where hundreds of deer often grazed protected and unafraid of human observation. For years the owner of the property had

prohibited hunting on the land, and the deer had flour-
ished.

Picketts also knew who lived there now: Diane Newton King. Something else also crossed Picketts' mind as
he sped to the scene: the threatening letter Diane had
received in her mailbox a few months earlier. Could it
be related to the emergency, he wondered.

As Picketts raced toward the scene, he listened for
additional details from the dispatcher. The information
was sketchy. A hysterical man had called the emergency
line seeking help for his wife.

Picketts, with lights flashing and siren blaring, sped
quickly past the Marshall Fire Fighters' ambulance that
was also responding to the scene. Picketts didn't know
what awaited him, but if it was a volatile situation,
he wanted to be the first there, before the emergency
medical team.

He turned his cruiser west onto Division Drive and
drove rapidly down the darkened, tree-lined road toward
the house. It was about 7 P.M. when he turned his patrol
car into the driveway.

A mercury light and a set of floodlights attached to
the porch gave an eerie glow to the area. Picketts could
see a Jeep Wagoneer parked near the house. Another
car—a station wagon—was parked several yards from
the Jeep.

Picketts drove slowly up the dirt lane. No one was
outside, an unusual situation considering someone had
called for emergency assistance, he thought.

The Jeep Wagoneer was parked in the driveway, facing
the house. The station wagon was parked several yards
away, facing the road. Picketts' eyes searched the barn,
the cement silo and the sheds adjacent to the house. He
saw nothing. He pulled his cruiser closer to the Wagoneer
and his headlights illuminated a woman's body. Picketts
recognized Diane. Dressed in a Desert Storm sweatshirt
and jeans, she was sprawled on her back, near the driver's

side door. Her legs were folded beneath her, suggesting she had fallen backwards. Her arms were outstretched. A set of car keys and a hair barrette lay nearby.

Picketts cautiously climbed from his car, his eyes continuing to scan the area. He could see a small trickle of blood around Diane's nose, but no other injuries. Her eyes were closed. He leaned down and felt her neck for a pulse. Her warm body yielded none.

Then he heard a cry, actually a wimper. He looked up at the Wagoneer. A youngster, still locked in his car seat, was staring out the backseat window toward the ground where Diane was laying. Tears rolled down the youngster's cheeks. Picketts stood up and shined his flashlight inside and saw another, much smaller infant strapped into a carrier, also in the backseat.

Picketts was then startled by screams coming from inside the house only a few yards away. He could see a man frantically waving his arms in the kitchen. Picketts stood up, motioned to the emergency crew which had now arrived to enter the area, and walked toward the house.

"Help my wife," the man screamed as he walked from the kitchen onto a porch. "Please help her, she's been hurt."

Before Picketts had reached the porch, one of the emergency crew members called to him.

"Guy, she's been shot," medical technician Jeffrey Caison said.

Picketts ordered Brad to remain on the porch, while he returned to the body. Caison pointed to a small caliber gunshot wound on the right side of her chest, just above the nipple. A small amount of blood trickled from the wound.

"We have a gunshot victim," Picketts radioed the dispatcher. "Send a supervisor and notify the detectives."

Picketts then turned his attention toward Brad, who had remained on the porch.

"I only have a shotgun," said Brad, who was wearing camouflage clothes, a cap and boots. "It's broken down on the back porch, by the washer."

"Is there anyone else in the residence?" Picketts asked.

"No."

"You stay right there," Picketts ordered as he returned to the area where the emergency crew continued to administer CPR to an unresponsive body.

"Try not to disturb anything around here. I'm going to get my camera," Picketts said, realizing he had to preserve the crime scene as best he could.

The discovery of the gunshot wound had heightened the tension. It was no longer simply a medical emergency, it was probably murder.

While Picketts was photographing the scene, Sergeant Harold Badger along with Deputy Lindsay and several other officers from various departments had descended on the scene. The cold, dark, Michigan sky was now illuminated by flashing lights that reflected into the eyes of the small child still staring out the backseat window at the swirling activity surrounding his mother. He continued to cry.

As the emergency crews attempted additional CPR, Badger noticed a second hole in Diane's clothing, this one in her jeans. The EMT's unzipped her jeans to find a second bullet wound, this one in the groin, just above the pubic area. It, too, trickled blood.

"Who's that in the house?" Badger asked, noticing for the first time a man standing alone on the porch.

"Brad King, the victim's husband," Picketts said.

Badger walked toward King and identified himself.

"Did you find her?" he asked.

"Yes, I went for a walk," Brad said, motioning to the fields behind the house. "When I returned I found my wife lying on the ground. That's when I called for help."

"Did you hear any gunshots while you were walking back there?" Badger asked.

"Yes, I heard shots off and on all day," Brad said, matter-of-factly.

Badger, a Calhoun County Sheriff's Deputy since 1973, was struck by King's nonchalance. He seemed too calm, and unconcerned about Diane or the two children, who still remained in the vehicle.

Badger ordered Lindsay to take Brad back inside the house and stay there with him. Badger returned to the body.

The emergency crews were loading Diane's body into the ambulance when Picketts looked up to see the barn loft door ajar. He quickly motioned to Badger. Instinctively, the two men drew their pistols and moved cautiously toward the barn. They opened the lower door and moved inside, shining their flashlights into the musty, dirty corners of the barn. In a tack room, adjacent to the main entrance, the officers spotted a chained Doberman pinscher. The dog was silent, offering no challenges to the officers' search.

The men then moved up the wooden stairs to the loft. They quickly searched the area, but found no one. Peering out the 12-inch opening in the loft door, the men agreed the shots could have been fired from there. The floodlights illuminated the area. The angle seemed perfect. Searching the hay-strewn floor with their flashlights, the men spotted a single spent .22 caliber rifle casing. Picketts took an ink pen from his uniform pocket and placed it near the shell casing to mark the spot. He left the casing there. The men then moved cautiously from the barn to the other buildings, but found no one.

Police continued to descend upon the King farm. A murder in Marshall was almost unheard of, and because it involved a local celebrity word had spread fast. Almost every high-ranking member of the Calhoun County Sheriff's Department was there or at least en route to the scene.

Inside the house, Brad had remained calm. He cooperated with Deputy Lindsay, openly answering any question the deputy posed. After Diane's body was removed from the scene, at least 45 minutes after the shooting was reported, Brad asked if he could get his children out of the car and if he could call friends to take care of the children.

Nuri Elgutta was waiting for his wife and daughter to return from an evening walk when the telephone rang. It was Brad and he was crying. Deputies at Brad's house were shocked by Brad's show of emotion. It was the first time they had seen him cry that evening.

"Barb?" he asked.

"No, this is Nuri, what's wrong?" Nuri said.

"Diane's been hurt," Brad said, continuing to sob. "She got hurt in the driveway."

"Stay right there, we're on our way," Nuri said, without waiting for Brad to respond.

Diane and Nuri's wife, Barb, had become close friends since Brad and Diane had moved to Marshall. Their friendship was grounded in their Native American heritage. For the past several weeks, Barb had grown increasingly concerned about Diane's welfare. Diane's attitude about herself and her family had changed drastically. At the first hint of trouble, Nuri knew Barb would want to be at Diane's side, regardless of what the problem was.

Nuri grabbed his young son, Dallas, and jumped into the car to find his wife and daughter, Ryan.

"Barb, Diane's been hurt," Nuri said to his wife, as he pulled the car to a stop a few blocks from their home. "We've got to get out to the farm."

Barb guessed instinctively that Diane had been shot.

"Nuri, I have a real bad feeling," Barb said, as she placed her daughter in the backseat, "but I'm not going to tell you what I think until we get there."

Barb began to cry as they drove in silence to Marshall, several miles from their home. As they approached the farmhouse, the flashing emergency lights confirmed Barb's worst fears. Now she began to cry uncontrollably.

"Nuri, she's been shot," Barb declared. "I just know she's been shot."

Barb looked over and saw the Jeep and several people standing near it. She immediately turned away. Although Diane had already been taken to Oaklawn, Barb didn't know that, and she was afraid of what she might see.

"Stay down," she told her two small children. "Stay in the backseat and stay down. I'll be back in a few minutes."

Not only did Barb not want her children to witness the horrible tragedy she expected to find, she was also worried about their safety. If Diane had been killed by a sniper, he might still be in the area. Her children could sense their mother's fear and they, too, began to cry.

The scene was a blur to Barb. Nuri had already approached a deputy who escorted him into the house. Barb, who had tried to comfort her own children before getting out of the vehicle, cautiously approached a deputy who stood near the roadway.

"Diane's been shot, hasn't she," Barb asked desperately.

"I can't say anything right now," the officer politely told her.

He didn't have to. The look in his eyes confirmed Barb's fear. She looked into the face of the young deputy, who gazed compassionately back at her. She knew he wanted to help her, but there was nothing he could say. She looked at the other deputies nearby. They, too, remained silent as her eyes met theirs.

"I've got to be with the children," she said to no one in particular. "Are they all right?"

The deputy nodded his head and escorted her through the maze of flashing lights and huddled police officers toward the house. Walking across the lawn, Barb refused to look at the Jeep, fearing what she might see.

As she approached the house, she could hear 3-month-old Kateri crying hysterically. The first thing Barb noticed as she entered the house was the two children sitting alone on the couch amid the furor caused by the constant stream of police officers.

She was furious. There was no one with the children. Two police officers were in the dining room discreetly discussing information they had gathered. Nuri was talking to another deputy a few feet away. And a fourth police officer was in the kitchen with Brad, who was routinely preparing a bottle for Kateri, a strangely mundane action in the midst of extraordinary events. He slowly washed the nipple and the bottle, gently drying it before placing the formula inside.

From Brad's actions, Barb immediately thought he was in shock. Then she became angry. He appeared so calm.

Barb looked into the other room where 2-year-old Marler was sitting on the couch, staring blankly across the room. He clutched his teddy bear. Kateri, who continued to screech, was lying next to him on a blanket.

Barb's first instinct was to go to the children, but Brad stopped her.

"Oh, Barb," he said, beginning to cry. "Oh, Barb."

"What happened, Brad?" Barb asked when Brad embraced her.

"Oh, Barb," was all Brad could say as he hugged her tighter and tighter. After a few moments, Barb pushed herself away, turning her attention to the children.

"I've got to go to the children," Barb told Brad. "We've got to get them out of here. I'm going to take them home with me."

She reached down and picked up Kateri, who immediately stopped crying. Marler blankly looked over at Barb as if he didn't recognize her.

"Marler, you're going to come with us," she said, gently patting his head. "You're going to spend the night with Dallas and Ryan."

Marler looked up at her and began to cry hard, deep sobs. She hugged him tightly with one arm as she gathered Kateri in her other arm.

The entourage moved outside, walking quietly past the deputies who remained in the front yard near the Jeep. Brad had picked up Marler and carried him to Barb's car.

The scene was horrendous. The painful shrieks of Marler and Kateri cut through the drone of police radio traffic with a piercing swiftness that affected everyone at the scene.

After placing his shrieking children in Barb's car, Brad walked through the throng of deputies to the Jeep Wagoneer, where he retrieved diaper bags and other baby items that Diane had brought back from Detroit.

Although Barb had assumed that Diane was dead, she didn't know for sure. No one had mentioned her injuries or her condition.

Barb held out hope that she might still be alive.

"Where is she?" Barb asked impatiently as Brad placed the items in the backseat of her car. "Where did they take Diane."

"She's at the hospital," Brad said. "At Oaklawn."

"She can't be alone now," Barb said, wondering why Brad wasn't with her. "I'll take the kids home and then I'm going to the hospital. Do you want me to come back here first and we can go together?"

"I'll meet you there," he said.

As soon as Barb and Nuri reached their home, she rushed into the house and called Oaklawn Hospital.

"I'm Barbara Elgutta and I am a friend of Diane King," she told a nursing supervisor. "I have her children at my home and my husband is taking care of them. I know you can't tell me anything about her condition, but I'm on my way to the hospital. She can't be alone. Where do I go?"

"Please don't come," the nursing supervisor said. "It would be better if you did not come here. Would you please hold, I am going to transfer you to the Calhoun County Sheriff's Department."

Again Barb was frantic. She couldn't control her crying. When the deputy came on the line, she again pleaded for him to let her be with Diane, to tell her exactly what was happening.

"I was just out there at the house," she said. "I have her children here with me. She is a friend of mine. I have to be with her. She needs somebody. Even if I have to sit outside, I'm coming to the hospital to be with her."

"Ma'am, please stay with those kids," the deputy said, without revealing the seriousness of Diane's injuries. "The children need you now."

"Is Brad with her?" she asked. "Is he at the hospital with her?"

"No, he's not," the deputy said, again pleading with her to remain at home. "Do yourself and the children a favor, stay with them. There's no reason for you to go to the hospital."

Barb hung up the telephone and began to cry again. No one had to tell her. She didn't have to hear the exact words. She had known it since the moment Nuri told her of the emergency. Diane was gone.

She walked back into the room where Marler was sitting. She could barely look at him. He seemed so alone and afraid. She wondered what he had witnessed, what he knew about what happened.

"Mommy fell down, Mommy got hurt," Marler later told Barb under gentle questioning. That was all he said. She hoped that was all he could remember.

* * *

Freida startled herself awake. She had dozed off watching television, and when she awoke it was almost 8 P.M. and Diane hadn't called. Freida was frightened. It was unusual for Diane not to call when she arrived home, especially after the threatening letter she had received.

Freida's first thought was to call and make sure Diane was all right. Then she decided against it.

"I should call, but I'm not going to," she told her husband, Royal, who also had fallen asleep watching television. "They probably went out for something to eat."

But the more she thought about it, the more anxious she became. She fiddled around the house until it became impossible for her to concentrate on anything else.

"Just call her and make sure she's okay," Royal said, more concerned about calming his wife's nerves than he was about Diane's safety.

When the telephone rang at the farmhouse, Brad picked it up.

"Brad, this is Freida," she said curtly. "Is Diane there?"

"There's been an accident," Brad said. "Diane's been hurt. I found her in the driveway."

"How are the kids?" Freida asked fearfully, her mind skipping immediately to her grandchildren.

"They're fine, they're with Barb," Brad said calmly.

"Where is Diane now?" Freida asked.

"She's at the hospital."

"Why aren't you there?" she asked, angrily.

"They won't let me go."

"Who won't let you?" she demanded.

"The police."

"I'm on my way up there," she said without waiting for Brad to explain. "We'll be there in a couple of hours."

Freida shook Royal, hazy from his nap.

"Get up," she said. "Something bad has happened. Diane is in the hospital. We need to go to Marshall, now!"

Brad shook his head in disgust as he hung up the telephone. That was all he needed—for Freida to be on her way to Marshall. The last thing he wanted was for her to be here bossing everyone around. He went back over and sat down on the couch, holding his head in his hands. Deputies swirled around him, trying to console him then alternately going to other parts of the house to discuss the case among themselves.

Shortly after 8 P.M., Brad received the official word from Deputy Lindsay. Doctors at Oaklawn Hospital had confirmed that Diane was dead on arrival at the hospital.

Brad began to cry. His shoulders heaved as he buried his face in his hands. He kept mumbling words that were inaudible to the lawmen around him.

"Is there anyone I can call for you?" said Jack Schoder, the lead detective on the case who had entered the farmhouse just as Brad was being told of Diane's death. Although they weren't close friends, Schoder had known Brad when he worked as a probation officer for the Calhoun County District Court. Schoder immediately felt empathy for him.

Brad looked up at Schoder and wiped tears from his eyes.

"Would you call Randy Wright for me?" Brad said, pointing to an address book that contained Wright's telephone number.

"Anyone else? A minister?" Schoder asked.

"Yes, Rev. Robinson," Brad said, regaining his composure almost as fast as he had lost it moments earlier. "His number is in the book, too."

Law officers have all seen people handle death in a variety of ways, but to a man, the deputies inside that farmhouse were dismayed by Brad's reactions. He acted almost as if he were one of them, a police officer notifying someone else of the death of a loved one. Brad was stoic to the point of appearing unconcerned.

Schoder and his partner, Jim Stadfelt, the only other detective in the Marshall police department, went outside to discuss what to do next. They both agreed that Brad had to be interviewed, and the sooner the better. Schoder agreed to conduct the interview while Stadfelt would attempt to get a warrant to search the property.

Schoder walked inside to where Brad was still sitting on the couch.

"I know this is very difficult to ask of you right now," Schoder said, "but you are the only one that was here when it happened. You are the only witness we have. We need your help. We would like you to give us a statement about what happened."

"I understand," Brad said. "I was a police officer myself for 12 years."

"Will you take him into town?" Schoder asked another deputy. "I'll be there in a few minutes."

Outside the farmhouse, Picketts and Badger were briefing Gary Lisle, a Michigan State trooper, about the murder scene. Lisle and his tracking dog, Travis, had been called to the scene in an attempt to determine where the assailant had gone after shooting Diane.

Based on the location of Diane's body and the shell casing found in the barn loft, investigators decided that at least one of the two shots had been fired from the loft.

After discussing several aspects of the case, including the fact that Brad said he had been walking in the fields at the time of the murder, Picketts directed Lisle and Travis to the barn loft. Once there, Lisle harnessed the German shepherd, a signal to begin the search.

The dog's tail immediately began to wag as his nose hugged the ground, an indication he had picked up a "fresh scent." Armed with a flashlight, Lisle followed

Travis down the loft steps, past the silo and into an open lane behind the house.

Travis, his nose to the ground and his tail in the air, moved quickly south onto a path that led back through the fields. Lisle, using his flashlight to follow Travis' movements, immediately noticed a footprint on the muddy path leading away from the house.

Travis followed the scent to a small creek, where a telephone pole and a piece of wood were used as a makeshift bridge. Lisle immediately noticed a wet heel impression that was beginning to freeze on the pole.

Travis, still actively pursuing the scent, crossed the creek and turned southeast into a brushy area where small patches of snow lined a deer path. Again, Lisle spotted footprints: one footprint was going north, the other pointed south.

Lisle thought the footprints were consistent with what Brad had told officers about his walk; there were prints going towards the house and away from it. Being cautious, Lisle radioed back to officers at the house that he had found footprints in the area that they should probably check.

Travis then moved quickly into an open field, still intensely following the scent he had originally picked up in the barn loft. As Travis followed along a deer trail, Lisle noticed another footprint, this time pointing in an easterly direction. It was similar to the ones he had seen all along the track.

As they neared the creek that wandered through the property, Travis hesitated. His tail began to wag rapidly as he entered the water. He again hesitated, then moved through the creek and into an open field in a northeasterly direction.

Unfamiliar with the area, Lisle followed quickly as Travis pulled him past a small power station and onto Division Drive. Travis continued to follow the scent west on Division Drive until he reached the driveway to Diane's house. At that point, the dog turned into the driveway where he immediately lost the track because of the amount of emergency personnel that had been in the area during the past hour.

CHAPTER 5

BRAD WAS CALMLY waiting in the break room when Schoder arrived at the sheriff's department in Marshall shortly after 9 P.M. Schoder had stayed at the farm to gather additional information from deputies on the scene.

At this point, the information Schoder had was sketchy. Schoder knew about the threatening letter, the telephone calls, and what Brad had reported as an attempted break-in at the house several weeks earlier. Schoder also knew about the elaborate security measures Diane had taken to protect herself.

Schoder also was aware of what Lisle had found: the scent Travis had followed indicated that whoever had killed Diane had circled from the barn, through the fields behind the house, then back onto Division Drive towards the King residence.

At the sheriff's office, Brad was cooperative. Schoder was prepared to be sympathetic and understanding. Although Schoder had interviewed relatives of murder victims before in his 22 years with the department, he felt uncomfortable interviewing Brad. He knew the interview would be a difficult task for both of them, not professionally, but personally.

Schoder suggested they conduct the taped interview in an adjacent squad room. The sheriff's department was abuzz as deputies moved excitedly about the small office, energized by the murder. Now it was mostly law enforcement officers, but soon they would be inundated with throngs of media representatives from around the world wanting to know why and how a local anchor woman had been stalked and murdered. The media coverage would eventually become as big a burden to the sheriff's department as the investigation itself.

Sitting in the small squad room, Brad was an imposing figure. His shaved head and camouflage clothing initially appeared intimidating. But a closer look revealed an introverted demeanor. He was emotionless.

Since Schoder considered Brad a key witness, not a suspect, he did not read him his rights.

"Brad, I guess we just need to talk to you to shed some light on what you heard or what you saw," Schoder said. "I know it's going to be difficult to go through it so damn soon, but why don't we start?"

During the next hour, Brad displayed a number of emotions, ranging from sorrow and self-pity to anger and frustration. All normal reactions, Schoder thought. What amazed Schoder, though, was Brad's ability to express one emotion after another.

Schoder's questioning initially focused on the obsessed fan theory. He wanted to know when Diane had left to visit her parents, when she was scheduled to return and who knew about her plans to return.

Brad explained that Diane had taken their two children to visit her parents in Sterling Heights, near Detroit, on Thursday and that they had returned earlier in the evening.

"I know her boss knew about it because she didn't do the news on Friday. Someone else did it," Brad said. "And her family in Detroit knew. And everybody she works with at the station knew she was gone."

"What about when she was going to return home?" Schoder asked. "Was that set when she left Thursday?"

"No, well, it was set that she was arriving back home today. But no time was set . . . I didn't know when she was coming home. She called me twice today. She called this morning," Brad said, breaking into tears.

"We can break here man, anytime you want," Schoder said.

"She said she'd be leaving after she talked to her cousin," Brad continued, waving off Schoder's offer to temporarily suspend the interview. "Then she called me later and said she wanted to spend more time with her cousin and wouldn't be home until later.

"And I said, 'Well, just let me know when you're coming home so I can have an idea of when you'll get here.' So, her mother called, I think it was about 4:30 P.M. and said Diane and the kids had just left . . . I had been lying down taking a nap when she called and I decided to go for a walk to kinda wake myself up. I usually take a walk back through the property whenever it's a nice day."

"How many acres you got back there, Brad?" Schoder asked.

"Well, there's about 500, but it's not mine," Brad said. "There's a lane back there that leads back to a creek, walk through the brush and come out to another lane."

"Yeah, sometimes I wish I lived farther out in the country," Schoder said. "So I can have some damn peace and quiet."

"Yeah, it sure is quiet back there," Brad said. He didn't realize he had just inadvertently triggered Schoder's first serious question about the evening.

"When you went for your walk, did you hear anything?" Schoder asked. Without waiting for Brad to answer, he asked another question. "Where did you go on your walk?"

"Across the creek, straight down the lane and through the brush," Brad said. "There's a deer trail out there. I followed that to get through the brush."

"Do you remember what time you went for the walk?" Schoder asked. "Because I don't have all the facts, you know. I was just called in on this. What time was it you took off on your walk?"

"Around 6:00," Brad said. "It might have been after 6:00, but it was around then. I walked back aways and then just kinda sat on one of those old bales of hay for awhile. It was starting to get dark, probably close to the time for them to come back, so I started walking back to the house."

"So you're just out there catching a little peace and quiet," Schoder continued. "How far were you from the house?"

"At least a half mile, if not more, closer to a mile? I walked quite aways. It's hard to judge. It was dusk, just starting to darken up. You could still see good though. I don't know what time it was. I didn't have a watch with me or anything. By the time I had gotten back to the house it had gotten a lot darker.

"That's when I saw her laying there by the car," Brad said, again starting to cry. "I ran over, grabbed her, called to her, shook her, and she was just motionless."

Schoder hesitated, waiting for Brad to regain his composure, but also thinking the obvious: what, if anything did Brad see or hear during the walk? Schoder knew Diane had been shot twice. Had Brad heard any gunshots?

"Let me ask you, and it's an obvious question, I'm sure you would've mentioned it to me," Schoder said, "but did you hear anything at all in the solitude out there?"

"No, well, I could hear the traffic from the expressway," Brad said matter-of-factly.

"That's it, huh?" Schoder asked.

"Yeah," Brad said, hesitating for the first time. "I, I don't know. I thought I heard what was a gunshot, but it sounded like it came from way at the other end of the property."

"And that's not unusual to hear out in the country," Schoder said, not pushing the issue.

"I didn't pay any attention to it," Brad said. "I mean I was hearing gunshots off and on all day today. People were rabbit huntin' or poachin' deer."

"Okay, so you thought you heard one gunshot," Schoder asked, knowing that Diane had been shot twice.

"Yeah, but I didn't pay any attention to it," Brad said. "I'd heard gunshots off and on all day . . . I just didn't think anything about it."

Although Schoder still didn't consider Brad a suspect in Diane's death, he found it strange that Brad didn't seem to think the gunshots were that important, especially knowing that Diane had been shot.

"Okay, let's try to work on the time here, as far as the last gunshot that you heard. How many did you hear?" Schoder asked.

"Just one."

"But you'd heard others while you were out?"

"I heard some when I was walking, but they all seemed to come from the same direction . . . I have no idea what kind of gun it was or how far away it was."

Schoder then turned his questioning to the time element, specifically, how long the walk actually took. Brad said he was about a half mile away from the house when he had sat on the bales of hay. When Schoder pressed him on the time frames, Brad responded:

"I don't know exactly. Maybe when my mind clears a little bit. I just don't know right now."

"But you didn't hear or see nothin' as far as walking up towards the house?" Schoder asked. "No car doors slam, no tires peal out, no engines running?"

"Nope," Brad asked.

"Not a goddamn thing?" Schoder asked, shaking his head in amazement, not anger.

"Nothing. It was totally quiet around there. Totally quiet, like it always is. My car was sitting there. I could see the Jeep."

"So, you went up and shook her and she was kind of motionless, huh?" Schoder asked as Brad nodded his head. "What did you do then?"

"I cried. I knew something was wrong with her. I called to her and then I ran to the house. I couldn't even remember the sheriff department's (number)."

At that point the interview was interrupted by officers wanting Brad's approval to search the area. He agreed without hesitation. When the interview resumed, Schoder changed directions. He moved directly to the problems Diane had had with the telephone calls and threatening letter, and what precautions she had taken.

"Over the last few days, or few weeks, has there been any strange activity at all in the neighborhood?" Schoder asked. "Have you noticed anybody driving by, or that you and Diane have talked about?"

"No."

"And she's not brought up (the letter) or had any more problems in the last few weeks?" Schoder continued.

"No. We would've been on the telephone with you if we had. We always tried to be careful."

"You guys have a pet dog?" Schoder asked, knowing that deputies had found a Doberman pinscher inside the barn where the shell casing had been found.

"More like a lover than a dog. It's still a puppy. She doesn't bark. If you walk up, she won't bark. She'll just jump on you . . ."

Schoder again shifted directions. He began to ask questions about Brad and Diane's home life, what their daily routines were and whether they usually stuck to the same daily schedules.

"Well, we're pretty routine, to tell you the truth," Brad said. "We tried not to be. There for awhile we were doing a lot of varying our things, but over time we just kind of lapsed back into doing routine stuff."

"So, if your car's there, you're there?" Schoder asked. "And if her car's gone that pretty much signifies she's gone."

"Yeah, that's pretty standard."

"Me too," Schoder added. "In fact, I drive my police car and my wife's kinda got her car. Our friends can tell who's home by whose car is there."

Suddenly, without warning, Brad broke down.

"Yeah, I don't know what I am going to do," he said, wiping tears from his eyes. "God, I loved living out there, but I don't know . . ."

"It's a difficult situation, to say the least," Schoder said, attempting to comfort Brad. "It's got to be pretty tough."

"I don't want to take the kids away from there, they love it. Well, my son loves it so much," Brad said.

Schoder thought it strange that for the first time since the interview had started, Brad mentioned his children. He hadn't said anything about them when he talked about discovering his wife's body or when the police had arrived.

Again the interview was interrupted, this time to inform Brad that his minister and other members of his church were on their way to the sheriff's office.

Schoder took a deep breath. So far the interview had provided him with little useful information. He still had many questions to ask.

"Let me ask you this," Schoder said. "Can you think of anything at all that might help us have an idea as to what the hell happened out there? Any indication or any feelings that you've been getting from Diane that . . ."

"No," Brad interrupted. "In fact, the last time we even discussed this problem was when she was home on maternity leave . . . We haven't had any problems at all for awhile."

Brad went on to explain that he stayed at home with the children during the day and that he hadn't noticed anything unusual at all. For the next few minutes, Brad rambled about what he had done earlier that day, including the work he had accomplished around the house. The interview seemed to be going nowhere. Schoder found himself stumbling over questions he had already asked. He was frustrated.

"So I guess what I am trying to figure out is what time you went for your walk," Schoder asked.

"Again, I did not look at the clock," Brad said. "I just kinda looked outside and said, 'Well, if I'm going to go for a walk, I better do it now. It'll wake me up and by the time I get back, Diane and the kids will be coming home and we'll go get pizza and have dinner.' "

When Schoder finished questioning Brad, he felt more dismayed about the events of the evening than he had before the questioning began.

Just as the interview was ending, the telephone rang in the squad room. Schoder answered. It was Diane's stepfather and he wanted to talk with Brad. Schoder handed him the phone.

"Diane is dead," Brad simply told Royal. "Someone shot her."

"We're coming up tonight," Royal said.

"No, don't," Brad said. "We aren't going back to the house. We're going to a motel. We'll talk to you tomorrow."

Schoder was struck by the coldness with which Brad had described his wife's murder to her stepfather. It was certainly not a normal reaction.

Schoder left Brad alone in the squad room and went to the lobby where several members of the First Presbyterian Church were waiting to talk with Brad. Randy Wright, Brad's best friend and his attorney, was also there. Schoder informed the group of Diane's murder and escorted them to the squad room to talk with Brad.

A few minutes later, Schoder again met with Brad and explained to him that officers were still at the farmhouse conducting a search of the area. He told Brad that officers were going to look for footprints in the area of the barn.

"Do you want my boots?" Brad asked, indicating to Schoder that he hoped that would help officers eliminate any of his bootprints that might be found in the area.

"Sure, that would be great," Schoder said.

In exchange for his boots, Schoder gave Brad a pair of jail slippers to wear home.

"We're going to get a room at the Arborgate Inn," Brad told Schoder. "If you need anything, I'll be there."

CHAPTER 6

THE FARMHOUSE WAS eerily quiet when Brad and Randy Wright pulled into the driveway about 10 A.M. Sunday. The deputies and the search dog they had used to scour the area in the early morning hours after the murder were gone.

There was no trace of the violence that had erupted the evening before. There was no yellow police tape marking the site. No deputies were there to prevent someone from entering the property. The murder scene was deserted.

Diane's Jeep remained where she had parked it. Brad's station wagon was nearby. The Doberman wandered quietly out of the barn as the men pulled into the driveway. The dog did not bark, instead it lazily wagged its tail at the two men.

Brad got out of Randy's car and slowly walked past Diane's Jeep, into the house. Stunned by Diane's death and numbed by a lack of sleep, Brad moved like a zombie through the downstairs. Reminders of Diane were everywhere: her clothes, the Native American crafts she had made and hung around the house, her makeup kit in the downstairs bathroom.

He thought about his children: Kateri's crying for a diaper change, Marler scooting around the house on a tear.

"It's so damn quiet in here," Brad said absently, as he rubbed his temples with his fingers. He stood in the middle of the room, lost in his own thoughts.

Randy thought it best to leave Brad alone. If Brad wanted to talk some more, he would be there. They had discussed almost every aspect of the case during the early morning hours at the motel, first between themselves, then with Diane's brother and brother-in-law when they had arrived at the motel early Sunday morning looking for answers.

The two men, Allen Marler, Diane's brother, and Donald Verrier, her brother-in-law, had met at Freida's home in Sterling Heights early Sunday. Freida, too distraught to drive to Marshall herself, had sent the two men instead.

They wanted answers, but Brad had few. After a 45-minute discussion, the men left, promising to return later that day. Not only did Brad have to worry about Diane's family returning, but his own parents and brother were arriving today.

Brad was living from moment to moment. He didn't know what he was going to do, how he was going to take care of his children or where everyone was going to stay. And funeral arrangements had to be made.

Brad also was concerned about the investigation. He thought it odd that the police left the area unguarded. The murder was less than 18 hours old, yet the police were gone. He wondered how they had completed their investigation so quickly. What had they found?

Randy went outside and started to unload the Jeep, removing clothes, diaper bags and the remnants of Diane's last meal from a fast food restaurant.

When Randy came back to the house, Brad was on the telephone with Barb asking her about his children.

"They're doing fine," Barb said.

"Great, we'll be over later this afternoon," Brad said. "I want to see my kids."

Shortly after noon, the telephone began to ring as word of Diane's death spread throughout the community. Many callers offered condolences, but others wanted answers about Diane's murder.

Brad had few answers and less patience. In most instances, he refused to talk, leaving Randy to answer most of the questions.

"We don't know what happened," Randy would tell the callers. "Diane was shot. She's dead. The police think it was someone hiding in the barn who shot her."

At Brad's insistence, the two men took the dog for a walk in the fields behind the barn: the same fields Brad had been walking in at the time of Diane's murder. It would be a chance to breathe some fresh air, Brad suggested.

The two men walked only a few hundred yards behind the house before it became apparent to Randy that he wasn't going to be able to go much farther in the dress shoes he was wearing. It was too muddy. Instead, the two men stood at the edge of the field, waiting for the dog to return. Brad attempted to describe to Randy his movements of the night before; where he had walked and how he had returned to the farmhouse.

"I don't know why I didn't hear two shots," he told Randy. "I just don't know why."

Shortly after the two men returned to the house, Father Jim Barrett arrived to offer his condolences and discuss the funeral arrangements.

Brad was obviously uncomfortable with Barrett. He found it awkward discussing funeral arrangements with Barrett because he hardly knew him. It was Diane who was the Catholic, not Brad. She was the one who had begun attending St. Mary's Church after they moved to Marshall. She was the one to initiate Kateri's baptism at the church.

Father Barrett also was uncomfortable, but he didn't really know why. He had talked to many people over the years whose relatives had died. But Brad was different. He showed little outward emotion, very little grieving. Brad showed the priest some pictures of Diane and the children, but avoided talking directly about Diane's death. In fact, during the 45 minutes the priest was at the house, the circumstances surrounding Diane's murder were never mentioned.

After discussing several options with Barrett, Brad stood up and announced that he was going to have Diane's body cremated and that she would be buried at Fort Custer National Cemetery in Battle Creek.

"That will be satisfactory," the priest said, indicating he could schedule the funeral mass for 11:30 A.M. Wednesday at the Catholic church in Marshall. The burial at the national cemetery near the television station in Battle Creek could follow.

A few minutes after Barrett left, Brad and Randy drove to Barb's house to see the children.

Barb didn't want to answer the doorbell when it rang. She was distraught over Diane's death and extremely nervous about seeing Brad. Although she had become close friends with Diane over the past several months, she barely knew Brad.

She also knew few details about Diane's death. When Brad had called her shortly before 11:00 the night before, he had simply said, "Diane's dead. Somebody shot and killed her."

Barb hugged Brad as he entered the house.

"Marler, your dad's here," she yelled to the boy who was playing in another part of the house.

The little boy raced into the room and jumped on his dad's lap. Brad patted his head, but said little to him. He didn't know how he was going to tell him his mother was dead.

At that point, it didn't matter. Within seconds Marler was off his dad's lap and into the other room to resume playing with Barb's children.

Barb was anxious for answers. But during the two hours Brad and Randy were at her house, Brad said virtually nothing about Diane or the nature of her death. Randy did most of the talking.

Barb felt even more uncomfortable after Brad left. Not only would he not discuss Diane or her death, he had spent very little time with Marler. He never once discussed how or when he was going to tell Marler.

"It was strange," she said later. "Brad didn't talk about Diane at all. Not a word. He ate pretty good. I couldn't tell if he was in shock. I didn't know what was going on."

As a counselor herself, Barb knew that people reacted differently to stressful situations. She didn't know whether silence was Brad's way of grieving, or whether he was simply indifferent to Diane's death.

"Something's not right," she told her husband after Brad and Randy left. "But I'm not sure what it is."

The two men returned to the farmhouse about 5 P.M. Although the relatives had not yet arrived, there was little peace. The incessant telephone calls, plus the reminders of Diane everywhere in the house, suffocated the men. The walls seemed to be collapsing upon them.

"Let's get out of here," Brad said. "Let's go for a ride. You want to go look at the deer?"

Once again, Brad wanted to go to the fields behind the house. If he was trying to escape the torment of Diane's murder, it seemed an odd place to go.

The men got into Diane's Jeep and drove out of the driveway, turned west onto Division Drive, drove past another house and then into a lane that led to the fields behind Brad and Diane's house. The field was extremely muddy, and within a few minutes Brad had gotten the Jeep stuck in deep ruts several hundred yards behind the house. The two men were forced to abandon the Jeep and walk back to the farmhouse, through the same area that Brad told Schoder he walked the night before.

Occasionally, Brad would stop to explain to Randy where he had been and what he had done on his walk the night before. It seemed almost like he was trying to convince himself of his actions. Or maybe he just wanted to cling to those last few moments before Diane's death.

Randy had been uneasy at the farmhouse all day, but with the encroaching darkness and the arrival of family members, he became increasingly nervous. He had read a copy of the search warrant affidavit left by deputies on the kitchen table, indicating the shots probably had been fired by someone hiding in the barn loft. Randy was worried about the attacker returning. Like everyone else, he didn't have a clue about who had killed Diane, or the motive behind the murder. But he was definitely concerned about the possibility of a second ambush.

Inside the well-lit house, Randy made it a point to stay away from the windows. He encouraged others to do the same.

"We don't know who's out there," he cautioned.

It was a house under siege. The unanswered questions and the mingling of the two families created enormous tension. Brad's family decided to return to the Arborgate Inn for the night. Diane's family, except Freida and Royal, who had decided to remain in Sterling Heights until Monday, would stay with Brad and Randy at the farm.

Anne Hill, a student at WMU, had just put her children to bed when the telephone rang at her apartment in Kalamazoo late Sunday night.

"Anne, this is Dawn," said Dawn Greive, a student and an administrative aide to Brad at WMU. "What is Brad's wife's name?"

Anne, startled by the question, had to think for a second. Before she could answer, Dawn asked:

"Is it Diane?"

"Yes, that's her name."

"Was she a broadcaster?"

"Yes, why?" Anne asked, confused by Dawn's strange questions about Brad's wife so late on a Sunday night.

"She's been murdered," Dawn said. "She was killed in the driveway of Brad's farmhouse in Marshall."

"What? When?" Anne asked.

"I don't know," Dawn said. "I just heard about it."

"You don't know when it happened?" Anne asked, trying to maintain her composure.

"No."

Anne didn't remember the rest of the conversation or even hanging up the telephone. She slumped to the couch. She knew she had to call Brad, but first she had to calm down.

Anne, a divorced parent in her mid-20s, had first met Brad in the fall of 1990 when she enrolled in his Tuesday night criminology class. She had immediately developed a rapport with him that extended beyond the classroom.

Throughout their relationship, Brad had led Anne to believe that he and his wife were in the process of getting a divorce and that he was making plans to rear his children alone.

During the fall semester, Brad had often shared his problems with Anne. And his problems centered around his estranged wife, his inability to get along with her parents and his ongoing financial problems.

"We were friends at first," she said. "I had told him things about myself that were very personal. He seemed like a very sympathetic, empathetic person who had dealt with a lot of tough things in his life. I thought he knew how to be a good friend to somebody who also had been through tough times. I really liked him."

In late October, the relationship changed drastically from friends to lovers. It was a relationship Anne encouraged, based on her belief that, like herself, Brad was in need of companionship.

She remembered the first time they made love. It was the day before Halloween, on a sunny afternoon in a park near campus. It was the beginning of a sexual relationship that was based on friendship and convenience—depending on one's point of view. For Anne it was friendship. For Brad it was convenience.

Thoughts and images of Brad raced through Anne's mind. The farmhouse, the driveway, the guard dog. She remembered the night they had made love on the couch in the living room of the farmhouse.

What had she gotten herself into, she thought, still sitting on the couch in stunned silence. Had he lied to her? Was he really getting a divorce, or was he simply using her for sex? She had no real answers. She was angry. She would never have begun a relationship with him if she had known he was still living with his wife.

Her anger was tempered by the fact that she didn't know all the facts about what had happened to Diane. She still liked Brad, and she wanted to be there for him if he needed her. She finally got the courage to call him.

Diane's brother, Allen, answered the telephone in the crowded Marshall farmhouse.

"May I speak to Brad?" Anne asked.

"May I ask who's calling?" Allen asked politely but firmly.

"Anne Hill," she said softly. "I work in the same department as Brad at WMU. I just found out about Diane and I wanted to call and express my sympathy to Brad."

"It's Anne Hill," Allen told Brad, holding his hand over the receiver.

Brad didn't want to talk with her. With everyone around him, there was nothing he could say. He shook his head no.

"Brad said he doesn't want to talk right now," Allen told her. "He will talk to you later."

Anne hung up the phone, her emotions swirling. She had so many unanswered questions. Did she have any information that might help find Diane's killer? She thought about all the things that Brad had told her during the past several months. Had he been lying to her? Was he truly a victim? Or had she been a fool?

She didn't know what to do or what to think. She would deal with those problems later. She tried to sleep, but she couldn't. It was going to be a restless night.

CHAPTER 7

B<small>Y</small> M<small>ONDAY</small> <small>MORNING</small> the national media had descended upon Marshall, hungering for the story about the local anchor woman stalked and killed by an obsessed fan.

But Jack Schoder wasn't sure they would find that story in Marshall. The more he thought about the stalker theory, the less he believed it. Although he had never investigated a stalker slaying, 22 years as a lawman told him the facts of Diane's murder didn't point to a killing by an obsessed fan.

Each time Schoder reviewed troubling aspects of the case, he found himself thinking about one person: Brad King. But each time he focused on Brad, he had to ask himself the obvious question: Why would he kill Diane? Schoder didn't have the answer.

Schoder knew Brad had found Diane's body. He was the only witness. He was the only person who had known when Diane was scheduled to return home Saturday. And most important, Brad's alibi didn't make sense.

Schoder also was intrigued by what investigators found during their initial search of the farmhouse on the night of Diane's murder. Inside the house, deputies recovered two boxes of .22 caliber rifle shells, several brass shell casings and a cleaning rod for a .22 caliber rifle. But

Schoder was more intrigued by what they didn't find: a .22 caliber rifle.

The autopsy Sunday in Grand Rapids provided detectives with additional evidence. The bullets taken from Diane's body suggested the murder weapon was a .22 caliber long rifle.

Schoder had several questions he wanted to ask Brad, but that interrogation would have to wait. Schoder was more concerned this morning with acquiring a search warrant for the farmhouse and adjacent property.

That's why Schoder had asked Lisle to bring his dog, Travis, and join approximately 15 deputies and volunteers in a follow-up search of the entire 500 acres surrounding the murder scene. If Brad was the killer, the murder weapon was probably hidden on the property.

By mid-morning Monday, Schoder had acquired the additional search warrant he needed from Magistrate Connie Wilkins. He had briefed deputies on their specific responsibilities at the murder scene and was preparing to return to the farmhouse when Brad appeared unannounced at the sheriff's office.

Accompanied by Randy Wright, his lawyer and friend, Brad wanted to know how the investigation was proceeding, whether the deputies had found anything during the search of the property early Sunday and whether he could be of any assistance to investigators.

Schoder was surprised and puzzled by Brad's unexpected visit. He prided himself on being able to read people. But Brad was difficult. He seemed so serene and so in control of the situation. His demeanor was not what Schoder would expect from a man whose wife had been murdered two days before. And it was even more puzzling to Schoder when he allowed himself to wonder whether Brad was the actual killer.

"Brad, can I talk to you alone for a few minutes?" Schoder said, ushering Brad into a small office adjacent to the squad room.

"Sure, what do you need?" Brad said.

"First of all, Brad, how are you doing?" Schoder asked. "How's the family and children? Are they okay?"

"We're getting by," Brad said. "We'll make it."

"We're going to do another search of the area," Schoder said. "We're going back out to the farm in a few minutes."

"Fine," Brad said.

"Brad, I'd also like to ask you a couple of questions," Schoder said. "First off, I'm having some problems digesting the information you gave me the other night."

"Specifically what?" Brad asked.

Schoder stopped for a few moments, gathering his thoughts. He wasn't sure how far he should go or what evidence he should reveal. He asked Brad to explain how someone could enter the barn without the dog barking or Brad becoming aware of it.

"You were in the yard all day," Schoder said. "If someone was stalking Diane, do you think they would risk entering the barn while you were there? Why didn't the dog bark?"

Schoder was also concerned that Brad had indicated he had heard only one gunshot instead of two.

"I'm as confused as you are," Brad said, shaking his head. "I've spent the past couple of days trying to figure it out myself, and I don't have the answers. I wish I did."

Again Brad was passive, gently deflecting any accusatory comments Schoder made. There was no animosity in his voice. He didn't challenge Schoder's inference that he was responsible for his wife's death.

"One other thing," Schoder said. "Could you draw me a sketch of where you walked Saturday night? I'm not familiar with the terrain and I'm having some difficulty understanding where you were."

"Sure," Brad said as Schoder handed him a piece of note paper.

While Brad was drawing the sketch, Schoder called Trooper Lisle into the room. According to the sketch, Brad had walked south past the barn to a large stack of hay bales at least one-half mile directly behind the house. He had then walked along the same path back to the house.

The scent Travis had followed from the barn, through the field and back onto Division Drive was different. Travis' tracking had followed a circular path, moving south, then east, north and west.

"If Travis followed the right track, you would have had to see whoever killed your wife run through that field in front of you," Schoder told Brad. "Don't you think you would have seen him?"

"I don't know," Brad said calmly. "I know what you're saying. I wish I could explain it. But I can't."

"Are you sure you didn't go over here?" Schoder said, pointing to an area east of the line Brad had drawn on the sketch.

"No," Brad said firmly. "I walked south, straight back to the hay bales. Then straight back north to the house."

Schoder shrugged his shoulders and handed the sketch to Lisle, who studied it for a few minutes.

"I hope this works out," Schoder said, patting Brad on the back as the three men walked out of the office together.

"Jack, would it be possible for me to get my boots back?" Brad asked.

"Sure, I'll get them," Schoder said, once again surprised by Brad's nonchalance.

The crowd of media representatives had continued to grow outside the sheriff's office. Satellite trucks lined the streets. Many television reporters were doing their noon reports live in front of the sheriff's office. Almost all were speculating on the stalker theory.

Brad didn't want to face the media. He asked Schoder if there was a back way out of the sheriff's office.

Schoder suggested Randy get the car and bring it around to the side of the building. He would take Brad through the garage and out a side door.

"Brad, there's one other thing," Schoder said as he escorted Brad through the garage. "Do you own a .22 caliber weapon of any kind?"

"I use to own a .22 rifle," Brad said. "But I sold it back in 1984 when we lived in Denver. The only weapon I own now is an old shotgun."

As Brad started to climb into the car, he turned and said: "I'm going to visit my children this afternoon. I'll be around if you need me."

The "posse" of volunteers fanned out a few hundred yards behind Trooper Lisle and Travis as man and dog began to search the property on a cool, bright Michigan afternoon. The wind, gusting at times, would hamper the search, but Lisle and Travis were ready. The two, partners since Travis was a pup almost 12 years ago, had run more than 800 different tracks together. Lisle was confident his old dog was up to the job.

The posse, volunteers that often helped the Calhoun County Sheriff's Department when extra manpower was needed, stayed a good distance behind man and dog.

Unlike the first search two days before, Lisle took Travis out of his harness to let him "free search" the fields behind the farmhouse. The footprints that had been so prevalent along the track two nights before had disappeared. The ground was muddier than Lisle remembered.

It was not long before Travis' attention shifted from the fields to the creek, along the same track he had followed two days before.

Travis stopped and excitedly wagged his tail while Lisle attempted to peer into the creek. However, the reflection of the bright sun shining over his shoulder prevented him from seeing into the trickling water. Travis continued to focus on the creek. Lisle took a piece of tissue from his pocket, tore a small piece and attached it to a tree next to the creek.

The tissue would act as a marker for the volunteers who were wading the creek a hundred yards behind them. Lisle radioed Picketts, telling him to pay close attention to the marked area.

After finishing the creek search with no other signs from Travis, Lisle moved to the lane where Brad said he had walked. He walked south down the lane to a small stack of hay, then continued south along the path toward the larger bales of hay where Brad said he had stopped.

Along the way, Lisle noticed two sets of footprints in some drifted snow. The footprints were pointed in the same direction, north toward the farmhouse. He saw none pointing south. Within moments, Lisle saw Diane's Jeep stuck in the mud. He realized the prints were those of Brad and Randy returning to the farmhouse after the Jeep had got stuck Sunday.

Back at the creek, Picketts and Officer Mike Shay were busy searching. Picketts, who had often waded the creek as a boy, walked along the bank. Shay, in hip boots, walked slowly through the cold, shallow water.

"Here it is," Picketts said, pointing to the tissue.

The two men stopped.

"Look, right there," Picketts said excitedly pointing to an area near the water.

The two men could see a 2-inch section of a rifle butt protruding from the mud. Shay froze, still standing in the creek. He didn't want to disturb anything. Looking down, he saw several spent shell casings lying in the shallow creek, near the gun butt.

Picketts immediately notified other deputies of their discovery.

Within a few minutes, Schoder and Stadfelt were at the scene. To avoid damaging any fingerprints, the deputies tied a bootlace to the butt of the gun and gently pulled it out of the muck.

It was a .22 caliber Remington Scoremaster rifle, stuck barrel-first into the water at the base of the west bank. The officers were ecstatic. Schoder's hunch had paid off. There was little doubt in anyone's mind that this was the weapon that had killed Diane.

Stadfelt, the detective in charge of property in the case, placed the weapon and shell casings in property bags. He was going to transport them to the state police's crime lab in Lansing immediately. There might still be fingerprints on the gun, and he also wanted to see whether the shell casings matched the casing they had found in the barn loft the night of the murder.

"We need to find Brad and get him in here," Schoder told Stadfelt as the two left the farm. "He's got some questions to answer. I'd also like to get his fingerprints."

Schoder never got the chance to call Brad. Shortly after returning to the sheriff's office, Brad called him.

"How did things go today?" Brad asked.

Although Schoder didn't realize it, Brad had been shaken by Schoder's questioning earlier in the day. He was anxious to find out what they had discovered during the search of the property.

It was not a reassuring telephone conversation. Schoder's mood had changed. His questioning was now more persistent.

"You need to come in," Schoder told Brad firmly. "I'm still having a hard time figuring out just where you were when Diane was shot. And I've got some other questions I'd like you to answer."

"Sure," Brad said. "I'm with my children right now. I just told Marler that his mommy is dead. I'll come over in a little while."

Schoder found it hard to believe that Brad might be the killer. As the father of small children himself, he couldn't imagine Brad murdering Diane for one over-whelming reason: If Brad did kill Diane, he would have had to have done it in front of his children. There was no way around that fact. How did it happen, Schoder wondered. Did he shoot Diane before realizing the children were in the car? Schoder couldn't allow himself to speculate any further. There was still a lot of work to do. Brad had not admitted anything, and there was no direct evidence to tie him to the killing.

But, Schoder thought, that might all change in a little while.

The media that had surrounded the sheriff's office all day was gone when Brad arrived shortly before 7 P.M. He was accompanied by his brother, Scott. Brad's constant companion since the murder, Randy Wright, had gone to Detroit because of prior commitments.

Schoder escorted the two men into the fingerprinting room. Brad seemed unconcerned.

"It's all part of the investigation," Brad had confidently told family members when the request was initially made. "They're just doing their job."

After the fingerprinting was completed, Schoder asked Brad if he had time to "go over a few things."

"Sure, anything you need," Brad said confidently.

"I would like to do it in private," Schoder said. "Let's walk down to my office. Your brother can stay here, if he likes."

The offices for the two Calhoun County sheriff's detectives were in a rundown building about a block from the main office. Schoder cleaned off a couple of chairs in the cluttered, damp facility called the Leyden Building. Schoder decided to be straightforward with Brad. Schoder also decided he didn't need to read Brad his constitutional rights.

"You are here voluntarily," Schoder told Brad. "You are free to leave at any time."

"I understand," Brad said confidently.

"I've asked you to come over here and talk about a couple of things and I appreciate you doing it," Schoder started. "But there is something that keeps going through my mind."

Schoder stopped mid-sentence and looked directly at Brad, who was seated upright in a straight-backed chair, his shaved head glistening in the dim light.

"Damn, Brad, you're the only person who was there that can tell me what was going on around there. You see what I'm saying?" Schoder said, initiating the interview with a challenge.

"You ask a question," Brad said, cutting Schoder off.

Brad had spent his entire life in police work and he wasn't about to offer anything to Schoder. He could tell right away that Schoder's questioning would be completely different than the "informational interview" he had conducted two nights earlier. Brad didn't know what the searchers found at the house, but something had changed Schoder's approach.

But Brad was confident that he was smarter than Schoder and better trained in interview techniques. He wasn't intimidated by the confrontational nature of Schoder's opening questions.

Schoder wanted to question Brad about several things: the time frame surrounding his walk; the number of gunshots he had heard; and the discovery of the rifle.

"Well, let's just summarize what you said Saturday night and then we'll go from there," Schoder said.

For the first half-hour, Schoder summarized what Brad had told him during the initial interview the night of the murder. The two men discussed how Brad had worked in the yard most of the day and later had rented and watched a video, *Next of Kin*.

Brad also explained how he had talked to Diane at about 12:30 P.M. that day. She had told Brad during that conversation that she would be home later than expected.

"I said, 'Okay, just let me know when you leave so I know when to expect you.' And she told me she would.

I said, 'Have a good time, love you. Hug the kids for me.' "

At Schoder's gentle urging, Brad explained that he had continued to work in the yard, lay down and napped for a while and then, about 4:30 P.M., received a telephone call from Diane's mother, informing him that Diane and the children had left. He told Schoder that it normally took approximately two hours and 15 minutes for Diane to drive from her parents' home to Marshall.

Brad also admitted to Schoder that he had been feeling lonely all day because he wasn't away from his family often.

At dusk—around 6 P.M., he guessed, he decided to go for a walk behind the house. The men discussed the length of time it had taken him to walk from the farmhouse to the bales of hay and back. Approximately one-half hour, they agreed. Brad also talked about hearing gunshots in the area that day.

Schoder stopped him right there.

"I guess the important thing here is, you did hear one gunshot," Schoder said, focusing specifically on Brad's walk that evening, not the gunshots he had heard earlier in the day.

"I heard only one gunshot," Brad reiterated, shaking his head. "I really didn't pay much attention to it. And I know there were two bullet wounds in her body."

"But you only heard one gunshot?"

"Right. And that is what perplexes me. Why didn't I hear the other shot?" Brad added. "Maybe it happened so close to the other, that I couldn't hear it."

Schoder stopped, shuffled his notes, then turned back to Brad, who was confidently looking back at him.

"I'm looking at some things here," Schoder said, shaking his head. "If you heard one gunshot when you got to the bales of hay, that would have been in the area of 6:15 to 6:20, by our calculations."

"Yeah?" Brad said, almost encouraging Schoder to continue the scenario.

"Well, Diane couldn't have been home yet," Schoder said, explaining the time it took to drive from her parents' home to Marshall.

"That's right. You're right," Brad said, seemingly unconcerned by the discrepancy.

"And now we bring it forward, you're walking back up here," Schoder said, pointing to the map Brad had drawn earlier in the day, where he had indicated he was on his way back to the farmhouse, "and you don't hear any gunshots. OK?"

"I just don't . . ." Brad said, his voice drifting off.

"See, Brad, that's where I'm getting messed up. I tell you Brad, I've analyzed this shit, man. I've looked at this up one side and down the other . . ."

"I can tell you're frustrated."

"I'm frustrated as hell," Schoder said, his face turning red.

"I'm frustrated, too," Brad said, almost condescendingly. "I know I'm in the area and I can't help you."

"Brad, I'm going to be real truthful with you. I've been in this business 21 years. You were in it 12. I'm being real truthful with you . . . I gotta get through this with you. I can't eliminate you as being a suspect."

For the first time since the murder, Schoder had finally said what he truly believed, that there was no stalker. Brad sat silently, waiting for Schoder's next question.

"I'm going to tell you another thing, Brad. And it's man-to-man here," Schoder said intensely. "And I'm not gonna pull any punches with you."

"I understand," Brad interrupted. "I don't expect you to. I just want the truth."

"Based on the information we have here, I believe you're involved. I believe you're responsible for this," Schoder said.

Brad didn't move. He showed no emotion. He simply stared blankly back at Schoder. Years of his own police training enabled him to walk delicately through Schoder's examination. At this point, he was in control of the interview. He was anticipating almost every one of Schoder's questions.

"I've worked on this for two days," Schoder said, his voice rising with every word. "I can't explain away a number of things. And I'm having a big problem, Brad, because I like you as a guy.

"Number one, we've talked to the relatives in Detroit, we talked to a lot of other people, and no one but you and the family in Detroit knew when she was coming home. You and you alone knew when she was coming home."

"I know," Brad said without emphasis or emotion.

"Second of all, you're out there in the yard all day. Twenty years in the business, man, a person who is going to sneak or stalk, whatever, is scared of being detected. You were there all day."

"I know."

Schoder continued his questioning, at times almost pleading with Brad to tell him what actually happened.

"I can't understand for the life of me how somebody could get into that barn with the dog being there. Now you say it's a friendly dog, and I observed that. It is quiet. But a person is not going to confine themselves to a building where they can only get out the front door with you being there all day.

"Diane's car has been gone during the entire goddamn day," Schoder said, his voice rising in frustration. "If somebody is stalking Diane, then what's happened, man, is they know you're there and she ain't. And you're telling me they're going to sneak in your barn while you're there and she's not?"

"That's what I would say," Brad said, surprising Schoder by agreeing with him.

"I cannot for the life of me explain away how you did not hear gunshots. I've been out there. I've been listening to voices and noises as they travel. I was out there at night. Brad, you would have heard the gunshots. There were two distinct gunshots. You would have heard them."

Schoder had crossed the line from simply questioning Brad about his wife's murder to accusing him of being the killer. Schoder leaned back in his chair and took a deep breath.

"Let me tell you a couple of things, Brad," Schoder continued. "I've been married for a few years and everything has not always been perfect."

"True," Brad said flatly, without expression. "Ours has not been perfect either."

"You've been receiving counseling?"

"Yes. We thought we needed some help to get back on track."

Schoder inched closer to Brad, a technique used in questioning to induce confidences. But Brad had been in Schoder's place before. Brad knew the tricks. He knew the type of questions Schoder was asking and what he expected Brad's reactions to be.

"I'll tell you Brad," Schoder said, "and you know this as well as I do. We're both adult men here. There is a fine line between love and hate. Sometimes you can cross over that line. You add up the pressures of life. You've got your part-time job, you've recently lost your job with the probation department. Some other things aren't going well for you.

"Brad, I can understand why things can fall apart and your wheels can come tumbling off, and I think that you probably need some counseling yourself . . . I think the wheels have come off and you're kind of skidding along. And you reached a point of total frustration. And you couldn't handle it. And I think you went for a long walk to kinda sort things out for yourself.

"I think you had enough psychological and mental pressures that just for a minute you snapped. You broke. And you lost your head. Brad, I'm really sorry about that."

Brad did not respond. Throughout Schoder's soliloquy, he had remained passive. Once again, Brad's knowledge of interview techniques enabled him to appear calm and confident.

"No," Brad said, finally disagreeing firmly with Schoder's statements.

"Brad, listen to me, man, you cannot go on with what happened there in your life without getting some help."

"Well, I know I have to see somebody," Brad said, implying that he needed counseling to deal with Diane's death, not his involvement in her murder.

"I'm talking about your involvement in this," Schoder said, frustrated by Brad's attempt to deflect the accusations. "I'm convinced you are responsible for this incident. I'm convinced to the point of proving it in court. We were out there this afternoon, Brad. We found the murder weapon. And we have other evidence of your involvement in this. Believe me, Brad . . ."

"I didn't do anything to my wife."

Schoder had confronted him with the most damaging evidence—the murder weapon—yet Brad seemed unfazed. He sat straight up in his chair, small beads of sweat glistening on his shaved head giving only the faintest trace of inner turmoil.

Unlike Brad, Schoder felt intimidated. He began to doubt his ability to get Brad to admit to the crime. He also began to question his own understanding of the case. Was he missing something?

"Just a minute, man, I'm talking about you," Schoder said, becoming increasingly frustrated. "I know that you did something that you would never again consider. But you broke down and you lost control for a few minutes.

"I don't know whether they call it insanity, or whatever, you just broke down and you lost control. And I feel it's important to you that you get some kind of help. It's gonna break you down and it's gonna shatter your total insides. Because what happened is not Bradford King.

"You understand what I am saying? We found the murder weapon in the creek. And we have more evidence. Okay? Everything doesn't happen in a vacuum. We have evidence that convinces me, and it's gonna convince other people, that you are responsible for this."

King didn't respond. He lowered his head and mumbled something inaudible.

"The gun is at the crime lab right now," Schoder said emphatically.

"I didn't do it," Brad said.

"Brad, let's go over this again," Schoder said. "You came down the track, there was nobody else down the track. You go over to where we found the gun. No one else has been over there. There is one person that went from the barn to where we found the gun. We can show that. There is no one else around there, except you."

"Yes, I was there," Brad said, his voice impatient.

"Is there any reason we should find a fingerprint on that gun that belongs to you?" Schoder asked.

"No."

"So, we just absolutely won't?" Schoder said. "That's fine. We went up to the lab today. I'm sure you understand that water doesn't remove fingerprints."

"Of course not," Brad said, seemingly irritated by Schoder's question.

Schoder hesitated, then turned and looked at Brad. He had been waiting all evening to ask this question.

"Would you agree to a polygraph test? I gotta have some answers. I gotta have some logic in this thing. Something has got to make sense to me. This doesn't."

"It doesn't make sense to me either, Jack, and it's coming out of my mouth. I mean if I were just some Joe Blow off the street that had never sat in your chair—you know, here I am talking to you, knowing the process, knowing about investigations."

"Okay," Schoder said without pursuing his original question about taking a polygraph test.

Brad had manipulated Schoder and the direction of his questioning, allowing him to evade the detective's question about the lie detector test. Throughout the interview, Brad had used his familiarity with police questioning to avoid pitfalls. Every time Schoder approached a sensitive area, Brad deftly moved away from the issue. Schoder didn't appear to have the experience to control the process. By now, it appeared that Schoder was intimidated by Brad's police experience.

"I'm sitting here knowing what I am saying doesn't make a shittin' bit of sense at all," Brad said. "I mean, there is a lack of logic."

"By your own admission?"

"Of course," Brad said. "But that's what transpired for me. Randy and I have talked and talked and talked—we don't have any answers. I keep asking myself why a guy would just sit and wait for someone. And, you know, I just don't have an answer for that. And I can only tell you what I know.

"Do we have someone who saw it happen?" Brad asked.

"Pardon me?" Schoder said, startled by Brad's question.

"I mean if somebody saw it happen it would be different," Brad said. "I wasn't there to see."

"We'll just have to wait and see," Schoder said. "I think we'll wrap this up for now, okay?"

The interview was over, but Schoder had accomplished little. He would be hard pressed to get a prosecutor to file charges based on the contents of Brad's statements.

The two men left the detective's office and walked silently back to the sheriff's office a couple of blocks away.

Brad was confident. Schoder was disappointed. He knew it would be the last time Brad would directly talk to detectives about Diane's murder without an attorney present.

Schoder was convinced he had the answer, but wasn't sure he could prove it.

CHAPTER 8

DIANE'S MURDER IMMEDIATELY transformed the proud, quiet village of Marshall into the scene of a feeding frenzy of journalists anxious to expose the world to the dangers of their trade—the stalking of reporters by obsessed fans.

Trucks with giant satellite dishes lined the downtown streets of Marshall. Television and radio journalists roamed the antique stores, coffee shops and taverns, desperately searching for the sound bite that would illustrate the horror and confusion the community was experiencing.

Diane's murder had all the ingredients of a great story: a well-known newswoman ambushed and killed by an obsessive fan in a rural town known more for its civility than its crime.

It was an easy story with national implications. Stalking laws were being introduced in state legislatures across the country. The only problem was that the story had been created by the media. Granted, Diane had been a television anchor, but her role was not regarded by her peers in southwest Michigan as a high-profile job. She read the morning news at a small station during local breaks of ABC's "Good Morning America." Yes, she had received weird telephone calls and a threatening letter, but the facts of the killing didn't lend themselves to the theory of a crazed fan stalking an innocent victim.

By Tuesday afternoon, Calhoun County Sheriff Jon Olson decided to set the media straight. Based on assurances by Schoder, Olson felt confident his office had enough evidence to arrest Diane's killer within days, if not hours. Although Olson couldn't specifically name Brad King as the killer, he would make it as clear as he could that Diane's death was not the result of an attack by an obsessed fan.

Olson called a press conference to announce as much. It was a mistake. The media's unquenchable thirst for details, coupled with Olson's inexperience in dealing with prowling journalists, led him to reveal more than he should have. Instead of simply squelching the rumors that were engulfing Marshall, Olson's comments would, months later, continue to fuel new rumors that would almost ruin the reputation of a local businessman.

"At this time, the investigation is starting to focus on an individual suspect," Olson told at least 35 reporters at a news conference at the Calhoun County Sheriff's Office the day before Diane's funeral. "We believe the suspect and the deceased were personally known to each other . . . I think we have the right individual. It now becomes a question of being able to convince the prosecutor and develop a case that won't blow up in his face. . . .

"This person is presently free to roam around in the community."

In an attempt to thwart what he believed to be outrageous misinformation about the killing, Olson had inadvertently frightened his community.

Marshall residents were used to attention—the city is well-known as a central stopover for travelers between Chicago and Detroit, and the annual homes tour attracts thousands to the community of 7,500. It is a community proud of its heritage. More than 850 buildings in Marshall are designated as National Historic Landmarks.

The thought of Diane's killer "roaming the streets" of the quiet town angered and frightened its citizens.

Across town, from Ken's Cafe to the historic Schuler Restaurant, the topic being discussed was Diane's murder and the fact that her killer was still at large. The hardware stores were doing a brisk business. Dead bolt locks were a high priority. Guns, a normal part of outdoor life in Michigan, were cleaned and loaded.

"We don't know what to think," said one elderly resident outside Ken's Cafe. "You hate to think it was someone around here that did it, but people are scared. You don't know what to think, or who to trust."

Olson's comments were based more on hope and speculation than on assurances from Calhoun County Prosecutor Jon Sahli. Although Schoder and Olson were "positive" that Brad was Diane's killer, they still had to prove it. And Sahli was already having misgivings about how the sheriff's department had handled the investigation. Initially, Sahli was told by members of his own office that the sheriff's department had made several mistakes in procedure that could harm the chain of evidence at any trial.

Sahli and Olson had had their differences in the past, and the sheriff department's handling of Diane's murder had done little to alleviate that. In fact, it had inflamed the animosity.

Olson's comments put Sahli in a corner. Although the murder was only a few days old, Sahli was already being pressured to make an arrest. If the sheriff's investigators believed they knew who the murderer was, why wouldn't the prosecutor file the charges, residents in the community began to ask. That question would haunt Olson and Sahli for months to come.

Even though the community was confused by Olson's statements, Diane's family wasn't. Although Olson had stopped short of specifically naming Brad as Diane's killer, his comments and Schoder's actions had left the family little doubt as to the main suspect.

The family had listened to the news reports on television Tuesday night and had read the newspaper accounts Wednesday morning prior to going to the church for the funeral. Now, they had to stand next to Brad at Diane's funeral. It was a circumstance that few people in the family could tolerate.

Outside St. Mary's Catholic Church, the cold February wind blew furiously against the backdrop of drum beats and traditional chants by the White Thunder Singers, a group of Native Americans that had been asked to participate in Diane's funeral. Some mourners performed the Indian ritual of sprinkling tobacco on the drums as they entered the church.

Incense made of sweet grass, tobacco, sage and cedar wafted through the air as hundreds of people silently filed into the red brick church. Near the altar, a table was decorated with a picture of Kateri Tekawitha, the first Mohawk woman to be beatified by the Roman Catholic Church and for whom Diane's daughter was named.

The camera crews, prohibited from televising the funeral mass, recorded every move outside the church. Brad, carrying an eagle feather, walked with Freida behind Diane's casket. He clutched her arm as the remainder of Diane's family followed them. An eagle feather was also placed in Diane's hands in the casket to "help her on her journey to her creator."

The funeral services were unique, a combination of Native American, Catholic and Presbyterian customs. Diane was Catholic and Brad was Presbyterian. Father Jim Barrett, the priest at St. Mary's, led the services assisted by David Robertson of First Presbyterian Church in Battle Creek.

"Diane was a vibrant person, excited I might say," Barrett told the congregation as sobs and muffled cries could be heard. "She was excited about her new baby girl, Kateri, her son and her husband. She loved her work. She loved the service she provided through her medium."

During the service, Brad occasionally dabbed his eyes, while Freida sat stoically next to him.

The next day, Diane was buried beside her father in Mt. Olivet Cemetery in Detroit. During a lunch following the burial, Brad was devoid of any appearance of sorrow or grief. He walked listlessly around the hall, occasionally chatting with Diane's friends, but mostly keeping to himself. The visible pain Diane's family was suffering was in stark contrast to Brad's behavior. His lack of emotion was particularly irritating to Freida. Her pain was now being transformed into hatred for Brad. She didn't want to see him or be around him, and she definitely didn't want him to have permanent custody of Marler and Kateri. Behind closed doors, the family was already making plans to have the children taken from Brad. And he knew it.

During the intervening 10 days, the family traveled to the Marshall area twice to attend Native American ceremonies commemorating Diane's death. Unlike Diane, most of her family had not embraced their Native American heritage. But even though they were not familiar with the ceremonies, they attended the festivities out of respect for Diane.

The first ceremony, a few days after the burial, was conducted at the farmhouse. It was difficult for all involved. Memories of Diane were fresh in everyone's mind. Then, on Feb. 19, the traditional 10-day feast was held at Julie and Andre D'Aratagna's home in Kalamazoo. At that ceremony, which like the first was conducted by Andre, Brad seemed morose, almost indifferent to the needs of anyone besides himself.

After everyone had left the gathering, Brad broke down and began to cry. He admitted to Julie and Andre that he didn't want to return to Marshall, that he couldn't spend another night in the farmhouse where Diane died.

"I just can't go back," he told them. "I keep thinking of Diane."

Although the D'Aratagnas had only known Brad for a few months, they felt sorry for him. And they loved Diane and her children. They let him spend the night, and a few days later opened their home to him and his two children. They told him he could stay with them as long as it took him to get his life back on track.

That weekend, with the help of several members of the TKE fraternity at WMU, Brad moved from the farmhouse to the D'Aratagnas' residence in Kalamazoo near the WMU campus.

It was the beginning of a new life for Brad.

CHAPTER 9

THE CAMPUS AT Western Michigan University was a haven for Brad King. It was a return to his past. His days as a student at WMU in the late 1960s were the happiest of his life. He had met his first wife there, and was named the Tau Kappa Epsilon fraternity's man of the year in 1969. It was an easy life then, full of promise and hope.

For a man now in his 40s, Brad's return to campus and to fraternity life—he became a faculty advisor to the TKE's—gave him a sense of fulfillment he couldn't find at home with Diane. There was no nagging at WMU, only admiration from students yearning to be like him. At WMU he was appreciated, respected. He was not "Mr. Diane King" at WMU. He was Professor Bradford King. The timid, introverted Brad King that existed in Diane's world disappeared on campus. Students flocked to his office on the second floor of Sangren Hall to talk. After his night classes, students surrounded him, full of questions about his life experiences. The discussions usually moved to local bars or taverns near campus where Brad reveled in the attention.

"I looked up to him as a father-figure," one student said. "I trusted him and respected his opinion. If I was unsure about something, I knew I could go ask him about it. He was always there, always willing to help.

Whatever his opinion was, I would do what he thought I should do."

"Professor" King was an imposing figure standing in front of his criminology classes. Tall, with broad shoulders and a shaved head to hide his receding hairline, he was in full control. To his students, he was a Native American, a Vietnam veteran, a decorated police officer and a separated, single parent raising two children alone.

In reality, he was an imposter and a liar. Worst of all, he was a predator.

Throughout Diane's pregnancy, Brad had walked a tightrope of deceit and deception—not only with Diane, but with his students. While Diane struggled with her pregnancy, the fears of being stalked by an obsessed fan, marital woes and the family's increasing financial problems, Brad was juggling a myriad of sexual adventures with several of his students.

"I always trusted Brad," said Kristine Overmire, a WMU student. "When I found out about his relationships with his female students, I felt violated. I felt used. He preyed on my innocence."

Overmire was one of several female students who had rejected Brad's advances, but others were not so fortunate.

In the month following Diane's murder, Schoder and Stadfelt found themselves bouncing between interviews with college students and Diane's family, friends and coworkers. But it was Brad's life on campus that most intrigued the investigators. It became clear to them that Brad had been leading a double life in the months prior to Diane's death.

Brad was a Tuesdays-and-Thursdays man. Those were the two days a week he could escape Marshall to roam the halls of WMU. It was on those days that female students could expect visits and telephone calls from Brad.

Two days after Diane's funeral, Schoder and Stadfelt drove to WMU to conduct a routine search of Brad's second-floor office at Sangren Hall. Although they discovered little of interest in his belongings, their appearance on campus fueled rumors of Brad's possible involvement in Diane's murder.

While most of Brad's students continued to stand beside him, others began to wonder. Rumors about Brad's affairs with students that had circulated on campus in the fall of 1990 now became prevalent. Students began to talk, not only among themselves, but to police. It was a break Schoder and Stadfelt needed. While the detectives had talked about the possibility of extramarital affairs being a motive in Diane's murder, it had been only speculation. In fact, as middle-aged men themselves, they had joked about the unlikely possibility that coeds would find Brad attractive. They were wrong.

Brad had an innate ability to make women like and trust him. In each case, his pattern was the same: he would befriend them with disarming charm and outrageous lies and then attempt to coerce them into bed with a sad story about being a single man trying to raise two children alone.

In some instances, Brad was successful in his sexual overtures. Other students flatly rejected his advances. But in most instances, the women he propositioned or bedded continued to admire him and to consider him a friend.

"He just seemed so honest, so open," said one student. "Even after he propositioned me, we still remained friends. It wasn't like a teacher-student relationship. It was more of a friendship. He was lonely. He was going through a tough time. Although I made it clear I didn't want to have sex with him, I still wanted to be his friend, to be there to talk to him while he was going through his divorce."

A few days after their visit to WMU, Schoder and Stadfelt received an anonymous telephone tip indicating Brad was having an affair with Julie Cook, a 19-year-old criminology major.

The detectives also learned that Brad had been cruising bars and the TKE fraternity house propositioning several women only three days before Diane's death. In fact, they learned he had had sexual relations with a female student three days before his wife's murder.

Through interviews with several students, the detectives were able to piece together a picture of an unhappy man whose central focus in life was his carousing at WMU, not his responsibilities as a husband and father.

Several students said they saw Brad and Diane arguing in the student center at WMU on Thursday, Feb. 7, the day Diane took the children and went to her mother's home in Sterling Heights, and only three days before her death.

"It appeared through her gestures that they were arguing," Heather Taylor, a student at WMU, told detectives. "Brad put on his sunglasses and was just quietly sitting there during the argument."

Heather was one of three coeds Brad had contacted that day. He had arranged to meet her for a late lunch after his afternoon class.

"He was unhappy. He just needed someone to talk to," she said later. "He was unhappy with his life. He was sad."

After his late lunch with Heather, Brad returned to his office where he met Julie Cook, another of his students. According to Cook, the two went to her apartment where they made love. It wasn't the first time they had made love, and it wouldn't be the last.

Their relationship had developed over the course of the past two semesters. First, it was a couple of beers and some simple conversation. Gradually it grew into a relationship built on convenient sex. Brad would call or drop by Julie's apartment, usually between his classes. Occasionally they went to a movie, but most times they met it was purely for sex.

"I felt attracted to him," Julie told Stadfelt. "But I'm not in love with him and he's not in love with me. We're attracted to each other. That's all."

Their tryst before his class that Thursday afternoon in February was normal. They drove to her apartment and went upstairs to her bedroom where they engaged in sex for about an hour while her roommates and their boyfriends remained downstairs. Brad then got up and returned to his office to prepare for class.

Brad made another attempt at having sex that Thursday. After his evening class, Brad was invited by several students to accompany them to Players, a tavern near campus. One of those students was Kelly Anderson.

What intrigued investigators most was Kelly's description of Brad. Like Heather and Julie, Kelly also described him as despondent, unsure of his future.

"He was kind of down, depressed," Kelly recalled. "He told me that his life seemed so complicated all the time."

At the bar, Brad made it clear that he wanted to spend the night with the 19-year-old student. His smooth, unassuming charm that had endeared him to so many students was gone. He was forthright, forceful with Kelly.

"He asked me if he could come home with me," Kelly told the detectives. "He asked me, 'So, are you gonna let me make love to you tonight?'"

Kelly said she brushed him off as she had done on numerous occasions in the past. However, as they left the bar around midnight, Brad again cornered her near her car. This time, he was even more adamant about his desires. His approach was physical, not verbal.

"He took me by the lapels of my coat and pulled me towards him," she recounted. "He looked at me and told me, 'I want to screw your brains out tonight.'"

She again rejected his advances and told him to go home. She blamed his actions on the alcohol. Ironically, like other students he had propositioned, Kelly didn't change her opinion of him. She continued to consider Brad a good friend.

"It wasn't anything I couldn't handle," she later recalled of Brad's advances. "And I really liked him as a friend."

In fact, when she learned of Diane's death, she innocently rushed to the Marshall area to be near him. She checked into the Arborgate Inn in Battle Creek and immediately called Brad at his house.

"I felt he needed my support," she said.

Brad told her he was with family and that she couldn't do anything for him at that time. He instructed her to return to the WMU campus and said he would contact her later.

She, like many other students, refused to believe that Brad was involved in Diane's death. She didn't know who had killed Diane, all she knew was that Brad was her friend and she would be there to help him.

When detectives interviewed Heather Taylor, she denied ever having sex with Brad, but did admit that he had propositioned her on more than one occasion.

She told the detectives she remembered seeing Brad on the Thursday before Diane's death. The first time was on campus when they had a late lunch together. It was apparent to her then that Brad was more interested in a sexual encounter than he was in her grades. Then, around midnight, she saw him at a TKE fraternity house party. As soon as he heard her voice, he had turned and started to walk toward her. Suspecting what he wanted, Heather avoided Brad and left the party.

A few days after their visit to WMU, the detectives also were contacted by another female student, Anne Hill, the woman who had called Brad at home after the murder. It was apparent to detectives that Anne was different than the other coeds they had interviewed. A divorced mother of two, she had initially thought that she and Brad were kindred spirits. She believed they were both single parents raising children alone. Unlike the other women the detectives had interviewed, Anne Hill sought out the detectives. After weeks of soul searching, she decided to tell authorities about her affair with Brad.

Anne was more mature than the other women Brad had propositioned. She was also remorseful. She felt used, somehow involved in Diane's death.

At a meeting with Schoder at the Kalamazoo County Sheriff's Office a few weeks after Diane's murder, Anne described a Brad King that now was becoming all too familiar to detectives.

She met Brad in the fall of 1990, while taking one of his criminology classes. At first she would stop by his office just to talk. However, in late October Brad asked her out for a beer after class. The two began to develop a friendship that Anne thought was based on trust and understanding.

"He told me he was a soon-to-be single parent who was raising his child by himself," she said. "I'm a single parent and I'm raising my kids by myself. We just established some common ground. He told me he and his wife weren't living together and that he had temporary custody of his son."

On Halloween Eve, the same day Diane received the threatening letter, Brad and Anne made love that afternoon on a blanket in a park near campus. Later, their encounters would usually occur at her apartment.

"We would always get together in the afternoon at my apartment," she said. "Always on Tuesdays or Thursdays. He would come by in the neighborhood of 2:30 to 3 P.M. and leave around 4 P.M."

In the early stages of the relationship, Anne thought that Brad was open and honest with her. He told her about his years with the 82nd Airborne Division in Vietnam, his work as a decorated police officer and his growing interest in his Native American heritage—none of which was true. He told her of his ability to kill, and the fact that death did not bother him.

"He told me he could disassociate himself from the feelings of death," she told the detectives about a conversation she had had with Brad. "He told me he had seen so much death that it just didn't faze him anymore."

But then the relationship changed. As soon as Anne began to cherish and nurture the relationship, Brad began to distance himself from her. He still wanted sex, but the compassion and understanding that had been the foundation of their relationship seemed to wane. He no longer wanted to hear about her problems.

Something else also happened in late November. One day Brad didn't show up for their usual tryst. When she confronted him at the university before classes that evening, he offered a startling explanation.

"He told me his wife had given birth to a baby that day and he had to be with her," she said, seemingly still hurt by Brad's dishonesty. "He told me he didn't know what was going to happen, if there was going to be a custody fight over the child.

"It was a tremendous shock. He had made it clear to me that he was separated and in the process of getting a divorce. At that point, I started to distance myself from him. I wouldn't initiate calls, and I would only go by his office if I needed something."

Although she tried to break away from him, it was difficult. Despite misgivings, she found herself longing for his friendship. She confronted him in early December about the future of their relationship.

"I just wanted to know from him if I should still consider him a friend or if he would rather that I drop off the face of the earth," she said. "He said that our relationship was becoming too involved for him so he was backing off. He told me he wasn't ready for another exclusive relationship like he had with his marriages.

"I told him that I didn't want a heavily involved relationship either, that all I wanted from him was friendship. I told him I didn't even care about the sex, I just wanted and needed a friend. That seemed to put him at ease, and we got back to the level it had been before the birth of his baby daughter."

The simple friendship didn't last long. A few days after that discussion, Brad called her at home and asked whether she would like to come to Marshall to spend the evening. He told her his children were visiting their grandma in Detroit. She agreed.

Anne arrived at his Marshall farmhouse about 10 P.M. Dec. 19. Brad was waiting for her as she pulled into the isolated driveway. She saw a large Doberman chained to a big tree near the house. Although it didn't bark and wasn't acting especially interested in her, she gave the dog a wide berth as she left the car. Brad proudly told her it was a trained attack dog and not to make any sudden movements.

"As long as nobody does anything threatening to me or the children, she's fine," Anne recalled Brad telling her. "But if anyone acts threatening, she'll break away and attack. She'd even attack the mailman if he looked like he was going to attack me or the kids."

Inside the house, Anne noticed the signs of a woman's touch. It was clear to her a woman was either living in the house or spending a lot of time there. A newly decorated Christmas tree with several presents under it was in one corner of the living room. In the downstairs bathroom, a hairdryer, make-up brushes and other female grooming aids were scattered around.

Before she had a chance to question him about it, Brad grabbed her and the two fell onto the living room couch, locked in a passionate embrace. For the next two hours, the couple made love in the living room. She stayed until about midnight, then returned to her home and children in Kalamazoo.

Brad seemed happy to see her leave, she later recalled.

The appearance of a woman's belongings in the bathroom again forced her to question her relationship with Brad and whether he had been telling her the truth. The more she reviewed the past several weeks, the more she began to question his honesty.

"He never said anything to indicate that he was living with his wife," she told friends. "But from what I saw that evening, it was clear she was living there, if not full-time, at least she still kept her things there."

Anne decided over the holiday break to distance herself from Brad. She loaded her spring class schedule on Tuesdays and Thursdays, making it impossible for her to succumb.

CHAPTER 10

NANCY RAPO DIDN'T know how to act or what to say. Not only was she worried about her own reactions, but she was also concerned that Allen, Diane's brother, would do something irrational.

Brad sat on their couch, assertive and in control. Allen shuffled uncomfortably in his seat, his eyes rarely leaving Brad's face.

Allen and the rest of Diane's family, after reading news reports and talking to Schoder and Stadfelt, had abandoned any belief that Diane had been stalked. They believed Brad was Diane's killer, and they anxiously anticipated his arrest. It wasn't easy.

In the weeks following Diane's death, Brad had become a different person. He was confident, smug, even angry. Not only was he angry with investigators, he was also seething over Freida's attempt to take Marler and Kateri from him. She had filed a motion in Macomb County probate court on Feb. 28 seeking permanent custody of Marler and Kateri. The court gave Freida temporary custody of the children, and also appointed her special conservator of Diane's estate.

While accusatory with Diane's family, Brad acted the role of the grieving husband with others, especially those friends living outside of Michigan—those who didn't know the details of the murder. While he never spoke of Diane around her family, it was a constant in his communications with others.

In a letter to a friend in Colorado, Brad spoke glowingly of his life with Diane.

"I still cannot deal with this loss," he wrote. "Diane filled a very big spot in my life. Everyone tells me it will just take time. I can't see that happening. When someone is so much a part of you as we were to each other, how can that ever be replaced? We talked about moving back to Colorado. I said to her that we left our hearts there, we should go back."

However, during the surprise visit to Allen's home in Detroit on March 7, Brad showed no feelings of desperation or remorse. He was irate and argumentative. He accused Freida of conspiring to take his children from him. He complained that he had not received notice of the custody hearing. He also accused Diane's family of blocking him from seeing his children.

"I'll get those kids back. There isn't a judge around who won't give me custody of those kids," he angrily told the couple. "The court wants them to be with their father. I'm not worried, I'll get those kids back."

At Allen's that night, Brad refused to look directly at his brother-in-law. He continually focused on Nancy, Allen's girlfriend. She was polite. She could hide her feelings. Allen couldn't. The fact that he believed his sister's murderer was sitting on his couch grated on Allen. He wanted to spring from the couch, grab Brad by the throat and demand that he admit to killing Diane. When investigators had first told family members that Brad was their main suspect, they implored the family to refrain from doing anything to jeopardize the investigation. The request made things difficult. The family was confused about how to act and what to say.

In a letter to Schoder the day after Brad's visit, Rapo expressed the family's consternation.

"I know many of the family wonder the same thing: should we ask Brad questions about what he knows of the case or if he has any feelings about who did it? I don't know if that would do more harm than good, it is difficult to figure out if Brad thinks we suspect him or if he thinks he has us fooled."

Something else bothered Nancy that night. She, like other members of Diane's family, was concerned that Brad might get away with the killing. As days passed without an arrest, her anxiety grew. His visit to Allen's home that night did little to ease those fears. Brad was cold. His actions and mannerisms did not come across to Nancy as those of a man grieving the loss of his wife.

After listening to Brad berate his mother-in-law over the custody battle, Allen attempted to change the subject.

"Hopefully things will calm down once the police catch the person and we can go on," Allen said.

"They won't catch him," Brad told him. "It's been four weeks and they have nothing. They won't catch him. I wouldn't be surprised if these guys have never even investigated a murder before. They are just small-time police. They won't catch him unless he kills again or gets drunk and shoots off at the mouth."

His words hit Nancy like a brick wall, especially his comment about killing again. She felt uncomfortable, scared. There was a definite air about him, almost a smirk, she thought. He was almost acting proud. He was not acting like a man whose wife had just been murdered. It was like a game to him, Nancy thought.

Brad continued to criticize Schoder and Stadfelt, and he bragged about his own experience investigating homicides while he was a police officer.

"When I was with the Pontiac force, I investigated about seven homicides," he told Allen and Nancy. "These guys in Marshall don't know what they are doing, they aren't really interviewing people. They only talked to me once that following Monday and they haven't talked to me since."

Brad wasn't only brash and assertive around Diane's family. He also exhibited those same characteristics when he returned to the WMU campus shortly after Diane's funeral.

Despite the detectives' investigation and speculation by students and faculty on Brad's involvement in Diane's death, Brad proudly returned to his WMU classroom. He carried a medicine bag and an eagle feather with him to class.

As he had done numerous times in the past, Brad blamed everyone else for his troubles. He accused the detectives of incompetence and of having a vendetta against him.

"They're mad at me for suing Calhoun County over my dismissal," he told students and friends at the university. "That's all this is about."

He also did something else: He asked some students not to mention to investigators things he had told them about his past. Specifically, he asked that students not mention to investigators the fact that he had claimed he was part Indian.

"In Calhoun County, they don't like Indians," he told Kelly Anderson, continuing to portray himself as a Native American. "They're out to punish me for something I didn't do because I'm a Native American."

Although he continued to communicate with the coeds he had had sex with in the previous months, he abstained from any sexual encounters. In fact, he avoided most of the students. Except for classroom talks and brief exchanges between classes, Brad kept to himself. He attended grief counseling. Occasionally he would let his guard down in front of the students, and his anger would surface.

"They don't have anything on me. They can't prove a fucking thing," Brad told Heather Taylor a couple of weeks after Diane's death.

After much discussion, Freida and her family decided now was not the right time to fight Brad for custody of the children. Although Freida had gained temporary custody, the family wasn't sure whether a court would grant permanent custody to them because no charges had been filed against Brad. Without charges, no judge was going to prevent Brad from having his children.

Shortly after Brad became aware of the temporary custody order, he hired an attorney and requested an immediate hearing. The court, at Brad's request, moved up the hearing from April 10 to March 18. At that hearing, Freida and her family withdrew their request for custody and let the children return with Brad to Kalamazoo where he continued to live with Julie and Andre.

"They didn't show up in court," Brad explained to a friend a few days after the hearing. "When they didn't show up, the court gave the children to me. Freida will not give me an explanation for why she tried to do this to me. As near as I can tell, the whole family was in on this. All I can tell is that they didn't want me to take the children and leave."

The situation was precarious: Freida couldn't keep the children from Brad, and he couldn't prevent her from seeing them. Their brief encounters, usually to pick up or drop off the children, were limited to topics regarding the children's welfare. Little was said about the investigation, and even less about Diane. It angered Freida, and her anger infuriated Brad.

In a letter to Regina Zapinski a few weeks after regaining custody of his children, Brad again chastised Freida and the rest of Diane's family.

"What I don't understand is why the children are so important to them now," he wrote. "They never made efforts to spend this much time with them, ever, when Diane was alive."

Brad was also upset that members of Diane's family had been talking at length to the media about Diane's death.

"I really don't trust anyone in that family. Freida says I won't talk to her about Diane. Well, I'm not going to until that whole family can keep their mouths shut with the media. I'm so angry and hurt that they did all the media stuff. It's a dishonor to Diane to do that. None of it was done in a way that Diane would have approved of . . .

"There are some days I hurt so much, but I keep going. Some people say it may take up to two or three years to fully (realize) my loss."

CHAPTER 11

BY EARLY APRIL, the consternation over the lack of an arrest in Diane's murder had reached fever pitch. Not only among sheriff's investigators, but with the citizens of Marshall.

"I think the sheriff's department is dragging their heels by letting the King case go on so long," said Marshall resident Lawrence Weeks in an interview with the *Battle Creek Enquirer*. "People are just out here wondering. The sheriff's department said they have a weapon and can connect it with the suspect. Then who is the suspect? You just don't let someone kill and then let them run loose."

Sheriff Jon Olson couldn't agree more. He was confident his detectives had identified the right man. He was ardent in his defense of his department, and even more adamant in his belief that the prosecutor's office was the one dragging its feet.

"My heart is screaming to tell who it is," he told reporters in March. "But my professional ethics will not allow me to do it. I don't want to see the prosecutor's case undermined."

Unlike Calhoun County Prosecutor Jon Sahli, who had made virtually no public statements since Diane's murder, Olson talked to the media at length. He thought it important to be open and honest with the public. He also thought it wouldn't hurt to put additional pressure on the prosecutor's office. He was frustrated.

"I would not change what I have released to the public," he said defensively during an interview with local media. "The family of the victim and the public have a right to an explanation, and to the extent that it doesn't jeopardize the investigation, I want to be open and honest.

"We are not any closer (to making an arrest) today than we were three days after the investigation started. The determination rests with the prosecutor. I don't know when the prosecutor will authorize the arrest of the suspect. It will depend on matters that are on his schedule. The prosecutor expects a finer-tuned case on a homicide than he would expect on a simple assault and battery or a larceny."

John Hallacy, an assistant Calhoun County prosecutor, tried to ease the tension developing between the two agencies and in the community in general.

He told reporters that, despite comments by Olson to the contrary, the two agencies were still working closely on the investigation. He reiterated the standard chorus of all prosecutors across the nation when involved in a tough murder case: it is one thing to say you know who committed the crime, but it is another thing to prove it in court.

"The lawyers know the law and what is required, and if it's not there, then we send it back for further investigation. We give the officers some guidance on what we think is necessary to prosecute the case," Hallacy said.

Even Diane's family was now publicly commenting about the lack of an arrest.

"We are not detectives. We are not policemen," said Darlene Goins, Diane's sister. "I'd probably be all over (the suspect) if I were, but sometimes it doesn't happen as fast as you want it to. Believe me, when they get somebody, I want them got."

Those were the prosecutor's sentiments. Sahli didn't believe the detectives had developed a strong enough case for a jury to convict Brad of first degree, pre-meditated murder. Despite the community upheaval and Olson's public comments, Sahli decided to wait. At each meeting with detectives, he prodded them for additional evidence.

That's where the rub was. The detectives thought they had presented Sahli with ample evidence to convict. In the two months since Diane's murder, Schoder and Stadfelt had spent almost every waking hour investigating the killing. They had traveled to Colorado and Texas, where they interviewed friends and relatives of both Brad and Diane. With the aid of the Michigan State Police, they had test-fired the murder weapon at the scene to determine the trajectory of the bullets that killed Diane.

They had served numerous search warrants, confiscating credit card bills, telephone records and personal letters. They had reconstructed a pattern of deceit and deception by Brad that they believed illustrated a motive for the killing. They were as confident now as they had been three days after the murder. They believed they had the right man and the evidence to convict him of first degree murder.

"I don't know what more they want from us," Schoder dejectedly told Stadfelt as they sat in their darkened Marshall office one evening late in April. "It's pretty clear who did it. I wish they'd just let us arrest him."

The detectives had learned several things about Brad that they believed showed motive. They knew that he had been having affairs with at least two women at WMU. They knew he and Diane had been in a constant state of warfare over money and her decision to quit her job in June to stay at home with the children. They also were aware of the turmoil between Brad and Diane's family. And they knew about the life insurance, approximately $54,000, that Diane had acquired through work at WUHQ.

Although detectives weren't sure that Brad had made the initial calls to Diane at the station, they had little doubt that he placed the letter in Diane's mailbox and that he had faked the break-in at the farmhouse to further enhance the belief that Diane was being stalked by an obsessed fan.

And most important, they had the murder weapon and Brad's own statements during the interview with Schoder. Brad's "soft denials," the inconsistencies concerning his walk behind the house and his inability to remember whether he had heard one or two gunshots left little doubt in the two detectives' minds.

However, prosecutors had a different view. For every piece of evidence the detectives presented, prosecutors could find something wrong with it that they said weakened the case. Prosecutors contended that Schoder and Stadfelt's case was disorganized at best. They accused the detectives of botching the investigation on several fronts, including the evidence gathered or not gathered at the scene. They thought Schoder's questioning of Brad was inept and would hurt their case more than help it, especially if taken before a jury.

Prosecutors conceded that Brad's affairs with the coeds were incriminating, but questioned whether they had reached the level necessary to cause someone to murder their spouse. Speculation about Brad having placed the threatening letter in the mailbox was just that—speculation. The detectives had found nothing specific to link Brad to the letter, prosecutors told them.

Sahli and his staff also were not quite as confident as Sheriff Olson that they could "place the murder weapon" in Brad's hands. Granted, the weapon had been found only a few hundred yards behind the house. But the weapon—a .22 caliber Remington Scoremaster Model 511—had been manufactured in the 1960s before federal law required a serial number. In addition, ballistics tests conducted by the Michigan State Police indicated that the shell casings found with the rifle and the one found in the barn loft were fired from the rifle. However, experts stopped short of saying the bullets taken from Diane's body had been fired from that same rifle.

"Due to the lack of sufficient individual characteristics or markings, I could not positively say the bullets were fired from the rifle, but they could have been," one ballistics expert told the detectives. The evidence was inconclusive and would give any defense attorney ample fodder to argue "reasonable doubt."

And most important, during his interview with Schoder, Brad had denied owning a .22 caliber rifle at the time of the murder. Sahli told the detectives it was up to them to prove that the rifle found in the creek was Brad's. It would be a difficult task.

Initial interviews with friends and relatives had offered little concrete evidence to tie Brad to the rifle. In fact, most of the evidence acquired by the detectives was circumstantial at best.

Brad's brother, Scott, told detectives their father had taught them how to shoot a .22 caliber rifle when they were kids, but that he hadn't seen the rifle in years and didn't know what had happened to it.

Brad's mother, Marjorie Lundeen, and his ex-wife, Gail Heitzker, also could offer little assistance to the detectives. Both admitted having limited knowledge of rifles, and neither was aware of whether Brad owned a .22.

After a picture of the murder weapon appeared in the local newspapers, the detectives received about 40 calls. However, few offered any leads. In fact, the only substantial leads merely added confusion to the matter.

Joanne and Mark Karaba, friends of Brad and Diane, contacted the detectives to tell them of an incident in which they had discovered several .22 caliber shells missing from their porch shortly after Brad had visited their house. That visit occurred only five days before Diane's death. The shells reported missing matched those found at the murder scene.

In addition, Thomas Darling, a Marshall businessman and a neighbor of the Kings, reported a conversation he had with Brad in late summer or early fall of 1990 in which Brad told him he owned a .22 caliber rifle and would use it to rid his farm of woodchucks.

That, in a nutshell, was the evidence they had gathered concerning Brad's ownership of a .22 caliber rifle. By any standards, it wasn't enough.

As the investigation dragged on, Sahli refused to comment publicly. But he was looking hard for help behind the scenes. Several weeks after the murder, Sahli, Jerry Woods, an investigator with his office, and Steve Houck, a Michigan state trooper, drove to Lansing to talk with members of the Michigan State Police, including a psychologist trained in murder investigations.

After briefing the state police, the group agreed it was possible Brad was a psychopath. They decided that an extensive investigation into his background should be conducted before any decision on an arrest could be made.

During the initial investigation, Schoder and Stadfelt had focused on the events surrounding the murder. They had spent little time delving deeply into Brad's past. After the meeting in Lansing, Sahli and his entourage decided to initiate an investigation on a much wider scope.

In a display of how the relationship between Sahli and Olson had deteriorated, Woods first discussed the trip to Lansing with Schoder. Woods suggested to Schoder that he contact Olson to see whether he would agree to bring additional people into the investigation, specifically members of a Michigan State Police task force.

Schoder agreed.

"If this is the direction he (Sahli) wants the investigation to go, I'm for it," Schoder told Woods. "But we need to all get on the same page on this. The important thing is for our bosses to get together because these decisions are not up to me."

A few days later, Olson agreed, and a task force was quietly assembled to re-interview everyone Schoder and Stadfelt had talked to. Within weeks, the scope of the investigation had widened to include not only Brad and Diane's immediate friends and relatives, but also people who had known Brad for years before his marriage to Diane.

CHAPTER 12

KRISTINA MONY WAS edgy about going to Brad's Kalamazoo residence. She hadn't seen him since Diane's funeral and wasn't looking forward to seeing him now. She was uneasy, but she couldn't pinpoint the source of her anxiety. But because of her anxiety, she had asked her mother to accompany her on this visit.

Kristina, a short, perky 18-year-old college student, had been devastated by Diane's death. Although Diane was several years older, Kristina had considered her a best friend. She had met Diane when she worked as a summer volunteer at WUHQ-TV in 1989. She later became Diane's assistant, accompanying her on assignments and even doing some interviews for her.

But theirs was a relationship that extended far beyond the television station. Diane and Kristina had become family, kindred spirits. Kristina babysat Diane's children and often attended powwows with Diane, Brad and the kids.

"I wish you were my daughter. You're closer to me than my own family," Diane had told Kristina shortly before she died.

Kristina admired Diane's tenacity, her compassion for people in trouble and her resoluteness in demanding that her children learn about their Native American heritage.

"Diane was a strong-willed, independent person," Kristina later recalled. "She might have been intimidating to some, but she would also give you the shirt off her back. She would do anything to help somebody. She was proud of her heritage, but she never was fake."

Kristina had also developed a close friendship with Brad. She remembered her conversations with him about boys and life, and how he always seemed to have the time to listen.

But now her thoughts were clouded by the dramatic changes she had first seen in Brad at Diane's funeral. She also couldn't help remembering a conversation she had with Diane on a shopping trip in early 1991, a few weeks before her murder.

While at the Lakeview Mall the day before Kateri's baby shower, Diane had confided in Kristina that she was having terrible difficulties with Brad and didn't know what to do.

It wasn't a complete surprise to Kristina. She knew the couple had been attending marriage counseling. In fact, Kristina had loaned Diane a book about relationships entitled "Secrets About Men Every Woman Should Know."

But Kristina was startled by the insecurity, fear and loneliness that she saw in Diane's eyes that day. For the first time since Kristina had known her, Diane looked helpless and afraid.

"Do you think I am attractive?" Diane had asked simply.

"Yes, of course," Kristina answered, smiling. "Why?"

"Brad doesn't," Diane said dejectedly. "He doesn't find me sexually appealing at all. He told me that."

Diane also expressed anger over the fact that Brad would not get a job and that he seemed satisfied to continue his career as a part-time instructor at WMU. Diane also was angry about the relationship between Brad and his daughter, Alissa, and wondered whether

Kristina thought Brad would treat Marler and Kateri the same way.

Kristina was also acutely aware of the fear Diane felt about the telephone calls and the threatening letter. Those fears subsided somewhat after Kateri was born, but Diane still took substantive precautions whenever returning to her farmhouse alone. Kristina had experienced those fears first-hand. Then came the horrible news that Diane had been murdered.

"He just had an evil expression on his face at the funeral," Kristina later recalled. "It just wasn't the same Brad. I didn't feel comfortable approaching him."

And she didn't feel comfortable seeing him now. Although she had desperately missed seeing Marler and Kateri, she had avoided Brad since the funeral. However, that all changed when he started leaving messages on her parents' answering machine in late March.

The calls surprised Kristina. She was unnerved, confused about what to say, and anxious about what Brad wanted. A few days later, she received a telephone call from Brad at her WMU dorm.

At first the conversation was simple, polite. Brad told her about his move with the children from the farmhouse in Marshall to Kalamazoo. They talked about his decision to attend grief counseling. He also criticized Freida for attempting to take the children from him.

And then he talked about the detectives and how he was their main suspect.

"It's just not fair," he told her. "I have these kids and I have to deal with all this other stuff. They (the detectives) just don't know what they're doing. They think I'm a suspect."

Brad went on to tell Kristina that he had hired his own private investigator to help him clear his name. He asked Kristina for her assistance.

"He'll be calling you," he told her in a voice that

sounded more threatening than she had ever heard Brad speak before.

Kristina had barely hung up the telephone when another call came through to her dorm room. It was the investigator, asking questions. Kristina didn't know how to respond. She hadn't had time to think about it. She hurriedly told him it wasn't a good time for her and suggested he call back later.

The investigator called again the next day. It was a brief conversation. Kristina was uncomfortable talking with the man. She didn't know who he was or whether he actually was a private investigator.

He asked generic questions concerning the suspicious telephone calls and threatening letter, the arguments between Brad and Diane and the problem with the IRS and the back taxes. He also asked her whether she had been questioned by the police. She said Schoder had interviewed her shortly after the murder. The investigator hung up and never called again.

A few days later, Kristina reluctantly decided to call Brad and see if she could get back the book about personal relationships she had loaned to Diane. Although she was hesitant to meet with Brad, she desperately wanted the book back. It was a piece of Diane she could always keep. They had shared many meaningful conversations about the book and it gave her a warm feeling knowing that she had shared it with Diane.

At 9 A.M. on April 11, Kristina and her mother quietly approached Brad's apartment with a keen curiosity edged with anxiety.

When Brad opened the door, it was immediately obvious to Kristina that he was a changed man. He was cold, distant. There were no hugs, no smile. It was the same way he had behaved at Diane's funeral. Brad escorted them to a downstairs area of the house where he lived with his two children.

Kristina was struck by Marler's refusal to come to

her. Instead, he clutched his dad's pants leg, almost shielding himself from the two women. The charismatic little boy with the gleaming smile had become insecure and frightened by the world around him.

After Kristina made several unsuccessful attempts to get a hug from Marler, Brad suggested Marler get his suitcase from a nearby closet. Inside the suitcase were all types of Native American items, from clothing and sweet grass to books on native traditions.

"I want Marler to know about his Native American heritage," Brad said. "We enjoy attending the powwows."

The women were struck by Brad's ability to distance himself from Diane. Her name was not mentioned and, to Kristina, it seemed that in Brad's eyes Diane simply had never existed. She choked back tears as she thought of the happy times she had with Diane and Marler at the powwows and how proud Diane was of her "special young man."

Now, looking at Brad and Marler, it seemed those memories were far in the past.

When he had called Kristina earlier, Brad had mentioned wanting to accompany Kristina to Diane's grave. He told her it would help his grieving process. He suggested they talk about it when she came by to pick up the book. But with her mother standing beside her, Brad didn't mention the visit.

Instead, it seemed as if he wanted their visit to end. During a lull in the conversation, as Marler played with one of the items in the suitcase, Kristina unthinkingly asked about the children visiting Freida. Brad responded in a cold, almost sinister voice.

"They might think they can walk all over me," he said, "but nobody will cross me. Nobody."

Kristina looked into Brad's eyes and felt cold chills run down her back. It was the first time she had allowed herself to admit what she had been unconsciously thinking since the funeral: Brad was Diane's murderer.

As she and her mother got up to leave, Kristina instinctively leaned over and hugged Brad. It was a mistake. There was no response. Brad never lifted his arms or attempted to make any reciprocal moves toward her. He simply stood staring at the women as Marler tugged at his pants leg.

As she walked out the door, Kristina knew two things: Brad was Diane's killer and she would never, ever, attempt to contact him again.

"He was a totally different person," she said later. "A totally different man. And it was more than you're going to expect because he lost his wife—people change when they go through a tragedy. It was more than that. He was a totally new person. It was definitely not the Brad I used to know."

But it wasn't only his demeanor. It seemed to her that he had physically changed. The weak, round-shouldered Brad that had followed Diane around with a "ducked head and puppy-dog eyes" had been transformed into a tall, arrogant man with a hard edge.

Kristina went home and promptly wrote Schoder a letter describing the encounter.

"The man I met today was not the same person that attended my graduation ceremony, the person who called to wish me good luck on Prom Night, or the person that sat at my kitchen table and ate strawberries with my family," she wrote to Schoder. "I met a man today that had gained a new strength and appeared to be in control and command of his life.

"This was not the husband and father we once knew, but a man that was capable of committing a serious crime."

Like many others, she knew the investigation was moving slowly and that the evidence against Brad was slim. Her decision to write Schoder was aimed at providing the detectives with additional information that could lead to Brad's arrest. But she was also realistic.

"I know that, unfortunately, my feelings don't hold up in court," she wrote.

As she finished the letter, Kristina began to cry. She thought of Marler and Kateri and the fact that unless something dramatic happened, they would probably be reared by the man responsible for the murder of their mother.

"It breaks my heart that Diane's beautiful baby girl will never know what a wonderful woman her mother was," she wrote. "She will never have her mother to confide in, to attend her school play, to help her get ready for her first prom, or to watch her receive her diploma.

"I hope and pray every day that you will find the monster that murdered my best friend. Diane King was a woman that touched many lives and had so much to share with her precious children."

Kristina was right: She wouldn't see Brad again. But it wasn't her choice. It was his. A few days after their encounter, Brad was making plans to move to Colorado with Marler and Kateri. Friends there, unfamiliar with the speculation surrounding Brad's involvement in Diane's death that was now running rampant among friends and relatives in Michigan, had offered him and his children a place to live and a part-time job.

It was an opportunity that Brad couldn't decline. Because of the ongoing problems over Diane's death, Brad did not finish his teaching assignment at WMU. He was replaced a few weeks before the semester ended. He needed a job. He couldn't rely forever on his mother's generosity. It also wouldn't hurt to distance himself from two very pressing problems: the ongoing scrutiny by investigators and the constant bickering between him and Freida over the children.

To assist him in his move to Colorado, his mother, Majorie Lundeen, had again provided Brad with money to escape his immediate difficulties. In a note accompanying a $2,000 cashier's check sent to Brad's credit agency, Mrs. Lundeen firmly instructed the agency how the money was to be used. She ordered that the entire check be used to pay bills, large and small, with none of the extra money returned to Brad.

"This is for all payments through September," she wrote.

The specific instructions didn't seem to bother Brad. When he took the check to the credit agency, he simply acquiesced to his mother's wishes.

"For a man who had just lost his wife, he didn't seem that upset," one clerk later recalled. "He seemed fairly happy, almost content."

That was the feeling that many who encountered Brad now had. Although Kristina and her mother, along with Freida and most of Diane's family, had been privy to an angry, resentful man, others had seen a different side.

"Brad was carefree, as if he had no cares in the world," Julie Cook, one of Brad's coed mistresses, later told authorities. "He was very upbeat. He was always outgoing and upbeat before the murder, but he appeared to be more relaxed after it. He seemed not to care about what was going on. He just seemed real nonchalant about everything."

Although Julie had rarely seen Brad since Diane's death, he did show up at her apartment in a drunken stupor about 2 A.M. during graduation week. He was admitted to the apartment by a roommate and went directly to Julie's bedroom where he stayed until about 4 A.M. He called again the next night, but this time Julie brushed him off, saying she was already asleep and didn't want any visitors.

The last time she saw him was in early June when they both took a graduate entrance exam. After the class, they had lunch and then went to a motel where they spent the afternoon engaged in sex. Like Kristina, days earlier, Julie knew it would be the last time she would see Brad.

"In my mind, I felt that we were spending our last day together," she said. "I was going back home at the end of June, and I got the feeling that he was not planning on staying around Kalamazoo much longer.

"When he dropped me off at my apartment, I said, 'Goodbye, have a nice life.' And he said, 'What does that mean?' I told him I just felt it was the last time we would be together."

She was right. A week later, Brad loaded up the Jeep with all his possessions, placed Kateri and Marler in their car seats and headed for Colorado. It was a place to which Brad longed to return. It was where he had been the happiest.

Once, during an attempt at reconciliation that had followed a heated argument a few months before Diane's death, Brad told Diane what he truly believed:

"We left our hearts in Colorado. We should go back."

Freida was worried. She hadn't heard from Brad in days, and her constant fear that he would take the children and disappear was always magnified when several days passed without at least a telephone call.

The relationship with Brad before Diane's death had been anything but cordial, and after her death it became downright hostile.

Freida, a short, dark-haired woman with a stubborn streak for a backbone, had been in constant turmoil since Diane's death. Initially, she was overcome with grief at the loss of Diane. Later, she became distraught over the possible loss of her two grandchildren. She knew the attempt to gain permanent custody of the children had been a mistake, made hastily at the urging of other family members.

Even after the aborted court battle, Brad had allowed the children to spend time in the Detroit area with Diane's family. However, he usually allowed only one of the children to go at a time, keeping the other with him to prevent Freida from trying to again take the children from him.

Often, Freida's only knowledge about the children would come from friends of Diane's who attended pow-wows in the area.

Since Diane's death, Brad had become painstakingly visible among Native Americans in the Michigan area. Many who were aware of the rumors about Brad's involvement shunned him at the powwows. But others, like Andre and Julie, seemed to encourage him.

Ironically, he was attending more powwows in the area and was more involved in the actual ceremonies than he ever had been when Diane was alive. He had also taken on a spiritual tone in his conversations. In a letter to a friend, Brad talked about his new-found enjoyment.

"I've found comfort in the powwows. It is a time that Diane is very present for me. I've been given most of an outfit and have made the rest. I dance with Marler. We say our prayers, put out tobacco and sweet grass and dance. Andre and Julie have been a source of great support for me and the children. I've made several friends from the Indian community over the past weeks."

Barbara Elgutta, Diane's close friend who had taken the children from the farmhouse the night of the murder, saw Brad at a powwow in South Bend. She was saddened by Marler's actions and frightened by Brad. Unlike his behavior with Kristina, Marler wouldn't leave Barbara's side.

"Marler was clinging to me," she remembered, "and Brad didn't like that. A couple of times, Brad was actually pulling on Marler, but Marler wouldn't let go of me, he kept clinging to my leg. It was obvious Marler didn't want to leave me."

Toward the end of the day, Brad walked over to Barb.

"He just picked up a chair and faced it toward me," she said. "He straddled it and just stared at me. He never said anything, he never talked to me. I think he was just trying to let me know he was there. It was scary."

Every time Freida heard the stories, her fears increased, not only for her children, but for herself. She knew Brad hated her, and she didn't know how or when he would react.

Then, on June 10, Freida's worst fears came true: She received a terse note in the mail from Brad, indicating he had taken the children and left Michigan.

"When you get this, the kids and I will be in the Denver area," he wrote. "I did not want to leave this way, but you set the ground for it when you tried to take my children. I feel I cannot trust you and had to leave this way to ensure that you did not try to do something again."

In the brief letter, Brad told Freida he would send her their address "when we are settled."

Freida was furious. She immediately called Schoder to inform him that Brad had left the area.

"I am sure you have the license plate number of the Wagoneer," she told him. "I would like very much to know when you locate them and what area they are in."

A few days later, Freida received another letter from Brad.

"We are in Colorado and doing fine," he wrote. "We are with friends and expect to have a place of our own within the next few weeks. I cannot give you the telephone number we are at right now given your actions in the past. I am writing so you will know that Kateri is with me and Marler in Colorado. Please, leave my friends out of your anger."

Within the month, Freida received another letter from Brad. This one was even more acerbic than other communications she had had with Brad since Diane's death.

Although he did give Freida a telephone number, the letter was demanding and threatening.

"I have heard through people in Michigan that you are concerned about the children's safety," he wrote. "This only further indicates that my concerns regarding your attempt to take the children are valid.

"There are two explanations that you owe me, and I will not stop asking for those answers until you provide them. One, why did you try to take the children from me? Secondly, why are you concerned for their safety? They are a product of the love and commitment that Diane and I had for each other."

In closing, Brad was adamant in his demands.

"The last thing I have to say is that you cost me $1,700 (in legal fees) over your trying to take the kids. That is money I can use. It was most of our savings. I expect to be paid back."

Freida, furious over Brad's demands and worried about her grandchildren, immediately called Schoder to find out whether he knew where Brad was living and what he intended to do. Brad's move to Colorado caused Freida and other family members to doubt whether Brad would ever be convicted. She questioned Schoder about that possibility.

"All I can say is that we are working on it every day," Schoder said. "We hope there will be an arrest."

CHAPTER 13

A TASK FORCE was quietly assembled without any media attention in late June. There were no press conferences, no promises to the public of renewed efforts on the part of the Michigan law enforcement community, nor any comments from Diane's family.

Although Brad's decision to move from Michigan had intensified the pressure to make an arrest, it wasn't the main reason for the increased interest by law enforcement authorities. Olson and Sahli were still unhappy with each other's behavior, but they had set aside their differences to focus on the investigation. They had agreed that the sheriff's department needed help if Brad was to be convicted.

Gary Hough, a Michigan State police detective, and Jerry Woods, an investigator for the Calhoun County District Attorney's Office, would head the investigation. Hough would be the administrator and Woods would be the chief investigator. Several other detectives, including Schoder and Stadfelt, would participate in the investigation.

One of Hough's first tasks was to organize the case into a manageable compilation of interviews and evidence. Schoder and Stadfelt had generated an enormous amount of paperwork related to the murder, but it was in disarray. There were pieces of information scattered everywhere, and if a conviction was to be gained, the evidence needed to be streamlined into logical groupings. It would be Hough's job to determine what information was important and how it related to the possible conviction of Brad.

The other main job went to Woods and his team of investigators. Within days, detectives from several Michigan law enforcement agencies were fanning out individually and in pairs, searching the physical and psychological landscape of Brad King.

For several months, beginning in late June, the detectives looked for evidence that investigators had initially either ignored or inadvertently failed to retrieve from Brad.

There were very few "fresh" interviews. Most of the people the task force intended to interview had already been interviewed by Schoder and Stadfelt. However, those interviews lacked the depth and scope that prosecutors now thought they needed to charge and convict Brad of murder.

Schoder and Stadfelt had worked hard. But in some instances, a second look at their interviews indicated a need for follow-up questions and answers. Their questioning of several key witnesses had been cursory at best.

By now, almost five months after the murder, it was clear to law enforcement officers that the conviction of Brad King would have to be based on circumstantial evidence alone. Brad wasn't talking, and the scene of Diane's murder provided few substantive clues.

The task force re-interviewed most of the law enforcement officers and medical technicians who were at the scene the night of the murder. They questioned them about Brad's demeanor, his actions to revive his wife and his comments about events leading to his discovery of Diane's body.

They contacted Diane's coworkers and friends, reviewing every angle, every possible scenario. The detectives returned to WMU, where they re-interviewed the female students who had earlier admitted to having affairs with Brad. Specifically, the detectives were interested in Brad's comments about his relationship with his wife in the months prior to her murder.

Although the basic elements of the interviews didn't change, it was clear that the attitudes of many of those being questioned had turned dramatically against Brad. The tenor of the interviews, especially those with Diane's family and close friends, had shifted against Brad. His every look, innuendo, and action over the past several months were scrutinized.

While the telephone calls, threatening letter, marital discord and Brad's affairs remained at the forefront of the investigation, detectives still searched for evidence linking Brad to the rifle. Without that evidence, it would be extremely difficult to convict Brad of murder. Schoder and Stadfelt's initial interviews had shed little light on the ownership of the rifle.

Brad had admitted that he once owned a .22 caliber rifle—a gift from his father—but he said he had sold the weapon in 1984. It was imperative for detectives to prove that Brad still had a .22 caliber rifle closer to the time of Diane's murder. They re-read all the reports, searching for any sliver of evidence that might link Brad to the rifle.

It was a re-interview of a close friend of Diane's— Barb Elgutta—that gave investigators the first break they needed: A witness who could definitely say she had seen Brad with a gun similar to the murder weapon.

Barb was scared. She had been frightened since the day of Diane's funeral. She had seen a different Brad that day, a more sinister Brad. But she had to talk to investigators. If she had anything that would help convict the person who killed Diane, then she had to come forward, despite her fears.

During initial conversations with Schoder shortly after Diane's death, Elgutta had said little about the rifle she saw in Brad's hands only weeks before the murder. But she surprised Detective Lou Mueller during an interview at Kellogg Community College when Mueller asked whether she had seen any weapons at the King residence.

"I saw one in November," she said, "before the baby was born. Brad and Nuri had gone for a walk, and when they came back in the house, Brad had a gun in his hand. All I noticed about the gun was its long barrel. I really didn't look at it that close."

Mueller then showed Barb a picture of the rifle recovered from the stream behind the house.

"Do you recognize this gun?"

"This gun resembles what I saw in his hand," Barb said, hesitantly. "The part that I see that resembles it is the long, skinny barrel. That's what I focused on when he held it. I couldn't really say 100 percent that this is the gun, but it resembles it."

Although Barb could not positively identify the weapon, it was the first time anyone had been able to place a gun like that in Brad's possession so close to the date of the murder.

Mueller ended the interview, but after thinking about it and talking to other investigators, he returned to the college the next day to meet with Barb again. He and the other investigators realized how important it was to get her to clarify what she actually had seen that day. Was it a rifle, or was it the shotgun that Brad admitted to owning?

"I just want to clear up a couple of points," Mueller told her when he returned to her office over the lunch hour the next day. "First, what is your basic knowledge of long guns?"

"I know the guns my father would use when he went deer hunting, how big and heavy and how long they were," she said, still hesitant but wanting to help.

He asked her whether she knew what a bolt was on a gun and whether she had seen a bolt on the gun Brad had carried that day.

"That's to open up the cartridge, or whatever you call it, to put the bullet inside, and then you close it," Barb said. "And then there's a safety on the gun, and there's other parts of the gun. I know what the barrel is."

"Okay, thinking back to that November day, Mrs. Elgutta," Mueller continued, "what was the type of gun that Brad had when he came in from hunting?"

"The gun that he was holding had a very long, skinny barrel. He had his hand over where the trigger is, and if there was a bolt, that's where his hand was. So I couldn't see if there was a bolt or not. I know it was a long, skinny gun. I was curious about it, because it looked different than the guns my dad used. My dad's guns were heavy guns, and I noticed Brad could hold it with one hand, comfortably.

"When I was talking to Detective Schoder, I told him I had seen Brad with a gun. I said it was similar to the gun my dad would go hunting with. I didn't use the word rifle because I don't know how to use the term."

"You don't know the specific difference between a rifle and a shotgun?"

"I can't tell the difference," she said, seeming confused. "I know the difference by looking at them, but I don't know the names of the guns."

Mueller showed her a picture of a shotgun.

"Was it like this?" he asked.

"No, it wasn't like that."

Like everything else in this investigation, her description of the gun had some flaws. She was not a firearms expert by any means and, although her description of the gun was similar to that of the gun found in the creek, it wasn't airtight. An astute defense attorney could focus a lot of attention on her uncertainty and raise numerous questions in the minds of a jury.

Mueller, although encouraged, knew they needed more. But he also knew he wasn't going to get it from her. She was trying to help, but she was also being honest. She really couldn't say positively that the gun she saw in Brad's hand was the rifle found behind the farmhouse.

Mueller only hoped that other investigators were having more luck finding someone who could positively link the rifle to Brad.

A few days later, another investigator on the task force, Detective Phil Mainstone, re-interviewed Tom Darling, a neighbor of the Kings at the time of the murder. During that interview, Darling was questioned about comments he had made to Stadfelt a few days after the murder when a picture of the rifle appeared in the newspaper. During the interview with Stadfelt, Darling talked about a conversation he had with Brad in late summer or early fall 1990 in which Brad admitted owning a .22 caliber rifle. Brad made the comment when discussing with Darling a problem he was having on the farm with a woodchuck. Brad said he was thinking of shooting it with his rifle. Unfortunately, Darling said he could never remember seeing a rifle in the King residence.

During the re-interview, Mainstone got the same response when he questioned Darling about the rifle again: Although he had been in the King house numerous times, he had never seen the rifle.

However, the following day, Mainstone received another call from Darling. He told the detective that he had mentioned the conversation to his wife and son at home that night, and his 15-year-old son, Christopher Sly, said that he had seen a rifle on Brad's back porch in the summer prior to the murder. Darling suggested investigators interview his son.

The next day, Stadfelt went to the Darling home to interview the boy.

Christopher told the detective that in the summer before Diane's murder he had mowed the Kings' yard. He said he had been in their house several times. He told Stadfelt that one day he was standing at the back door, waiting to get paid, when he noticed a weapon lying on top of a freezer on the back porch.

"Do you know the difference between a shotgun and a rifle?" Stadfelt asked.

"Yes."

"Is there anything you can recall about the particular weapon that you saw on the freezer?" he asked.

"No. I just remember how it loaded and that it was a rifle. And it was on the freezer."

"When Mr. King came to the door, did he mention anything about the gun being out there?"

"No. It was just sitting there on the freezer. There was nothing strange about it."

Christopher indicated it was definitely a rifle, but like the others, he couldn't say positively that the rifle recovered from the creek was the same weapon.

Christopher's comments were helpful, but not entirely conclusive. Stadfelt returned to the sheriff's office in Marshall encouraged, but not overly enthusiastic about Chris's testimony, especially since the information had been given to detectives several months after the murder.

The investigators agreed the case was much stronger because of the additional interviews, but they still didn't have conclusive evidence that the rifle belonged to Brad. They wanted more but weren't sure they would get it. At some point, prosecutors were simply going to have to decide whether to pursue the prosecution or disband the task force and hope that a break came later.

*   *   *

Sahli wasn't ready to quit. It wasn't a lack of effort that had stalled the investigation. It was a lack of evidence. Sahli and his staff were determined to get more.

In early December, Sahli, Woods and Hough quietly traveled to Denver to continue their investigation of Brad. Schoder and Stadfelt were briefed on the trip, but remained in Marshall.

Based on evidence investigators had acquired during the past eight months, Sahli asked authorities in Denver to issue a seach warrant for Brad's residence.

The affidavit accompanying the search warrant revealed the initial investigation to be shabby at best. Much of the evidence authorities were now seeking had been in the hands of detectives within days of the killing, if not the night of the killing.

Specifically, investigators searched Brad's apartment for a gun cabinet, gun-cleaning equipment and .22 caliber shells. They also were looking for any evidence that might document Brad's ownership of a .22 caliber rifle. Although they found several of the items indicated on the search warrant, they didn't turn up any information demonstrating that Brad owned a rifle.

While at the apartment, detectives discovered additional items, including camouflage clothing and boots that looked like the ones Brad was wearing the night of Diane's death. Because those items were not listed on the original search warrant, the detectives returned the next day with a second search warrant to confiscate those items.

Throughout the entire process, Brad remained stoic. He showed little emotion and didn't interfere as the detectives searched his belongings. He was calm, almost distant in his response to the invasion.

The next day, Sahli, Woods and Hough returned to Michigan, hoping it would be only a matter of time before they could arrest Brad for Diane's murder.

Although the investigators hadn't gotten a confession—Brad refused to discuss the case with them—and they couldn't positively tie Brad to the weapon, they did feel confident that they had covered every possible avenue. Sahli knew the case would be difficult to prosecute, but based on the additional investigation over the summer, the search warrants they had used in Colorado and the belief that they had built a scenario a jury could understand, he felt comfortable in proceeding with the arrest.

It was now a matter of timing, Sahli told confidants upon his return to Michigan. In the minds of the detectives, the question now was when Brad would be charged with murder, not if.

While prosecutors and detectives quietly worked on the Diane King murder case, Marshall residents carried on their own rumor-filled discussions about the murder. By early 1992, the rumors had reached a fever pitch. Tom Darling, the owner of a hardware store in Marshall, was at the center of one rumor. Without any basis in fact, the rumor of Darling's involvement in the murder fueled speculation that Diane had been killed because of a lover's quarrel. It was a rumor that police spent little time investigating, primarily because the facts indicated Darling simply couldn't have done it. He and his family had been on a church outing several hundred miles away at the time of Diane's death. Despite that fact, the rumors about him did not subside.

Although Darling and his family had been interviewed numerous times by detectives in connection with the murder, his involvement in the case was as a material witness, not a suspect.

The rumor involving Darling was the result of gossip concerning Brad's sexual escapades. As word of Brad's affairs with WMU coeds spread, it wasn't long before people in the community took it upon themselves to also

Diane Newton King in a modeling photo a few months
before her murder in 1991.   *(Battle Creek Enquirer)*

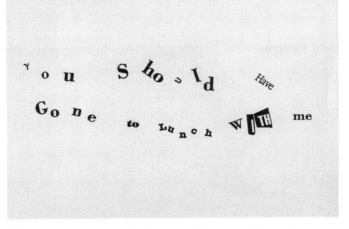

The threatening note Brad sent to Diane, which made her believe she was being stalked by a crazed fan.

(Calhoun County Sheriff's Department)

Jurors visit the farmhouse and property where Diane was found shot.

(Battle Creek Enquirer)

Freida Newton, Diane's mother, standing beside Brad King at the funeral in February 1991. *(Battle Creek Enquirer)*

Brad King arriving at the Kalamazoo/Battle Creek Airport after being extradited from Colorado. *(Battle Creek Enquirer)*

Brad King with his first defense attorney, James Brady, at his arraignment in February 1992. *(Battle Creek Enquirer)*

Julie Cook testifying at the trial.
(Battle Creek Enquirer)

Detective Jack Schoder of the Calhoun County Sheriff's Department. *(Battle Creek Enquirer)*

Detective Jim Stadfelt of the Calhoun County Sheriff's Department holding the murder weapon at the trial. *(Battle Creek Enquirer)*

Prosecutor Jon Sahli.
(Battle Creek Enquirer)

Brad King's defense
attorney at the trial,
John Sims.
(Battle Creek Enquirer)

Brad King, center, confers with his lawyers, John Sims and
Virginia Cairns, at his trial.   *(Battle Creek Enquirer)*

impute Diane's reputation. The lifestyle of the attractive, high-profile anchorwoman was at the center of the speculation.

Other scandalous rumors, fueled by comments about Diane's love life, even questioned the paternity of Kateri. That was due in part to an off-hand comment made by a lawman involved in the investigation. During an interview with a student at WMU early in the investigation, the coed had told detectives that Brad had implied that Kateri was the result of an affair Diane had while the couple was estranged. True, Brad made the statement, but only to further his own needs: keeping his young mistresses believing that he was the discarded mate, not Diane. Later he told the girl the truth—that Kateri was his child.

Regardless, the rumors continued to swirl. As the weeks, then months, dragged on, people in Marshall began to squirm with uneasiness. Some residents professed to know the "real story," while others simply continued to spread the latest gossip without regard for the family and friends of those caught in the web of small-town speculation. On one day alone, the sheriff's department received almost 50 inquiries from residents wanting to know whether the rumor about Tom Darling was true.

It became so bad that Olson and Sahli were forced to issue a joint press release to squelch the rumor. The terse press release indicated two things: No arrests had been made and Tom Darling was not a suspect.

The sheriff's department wasn't the only one overwhelmed by the rumors. Journalists throughout the region were kept busy trying to follow up on all the speculation. The *Battle Creek Enquirer* was forced to deal with the rumors in an editorial. The newspaper not only attempted to squelch the gossip, they also criticized local authorities for adding fuel to the rumors by their continued silence.

"Those probing the case refuse to release any data other than to say the investigation continues," the Jan. 26 editorial stated. "Until this information blackout is lifted, rumors will thrive—along with the inherent, perhaps unfounded, fear that a killer remains among us.

"Let's end the official silence. People deserve to know. Otherwise, they may go back to making up their own solutions."

CHAPTER 14

THE DAY BRAD had feared and Diane's family had hoped for finally arrived on Friday, Jan. 30, 1992.

About 9:30 A.M., as Brad was driving out of his southeast Denver apartment complex with his two small children, Colorado lawmen stopped his car and placed him in custody on a Michigan arrest warrant charging him with open murder and possession of a firearm in the commission of a felony.

Brad offered no resistance. The children were placed in protective custody awaiting a determination by Colorado courts regarding their custody. Brad was taken to the city jail, where he was held without bond, pending an extradition hearing.

"It was almost like he expected it," said one lawman involved in the arrest. "He was cool. Not upset at all."

Several hundred miles away, Sahli and Olson held a joint press conference in which they announced the "arrest of a man in connection with Diane's murder." As had been Sahli's practice throughout the investigation, the press conference was cloaked in secrecy. Although he announced the arrest of a suspect, Sahli refused to release the man's name, pending his first court appearance in Colorado.

Sahli also refused to say why it had taken so long for the man's arrest—almost one year—and why he had decided to issue the warrant now. During intense questioning by journalists, the diminutive Sahli fought off the questions with a simple, terse answer:

"I was ready," he said dryly. "I have been spending the last couple of weeks reviewing it and decided Thursday afternoon to issue the warrant."

That was it. He was ready. There were no long-winded explanations about the difficult nature of the case, or his belief that the initial investigation had been botched.

"The case will become clear in court," he told a small group of reporters after the press conference had ended.

While Sahli and Olson refused to comment on the events leading to Brad's arrest, lawmen in Denver weren't nearly so reticent.

"He was in the process of moving," Sergeant Doug Hildebrandt, a Denver police officer, told reporters. "He was being evicted from his apartment and was picking up some of his things."

Although Sahli and Olson refused to name the suspect during the Friday press conference, it wasn't a surprise to anyone who knew anything about the case. Most of the reporters there were fully aware that Brad had been arrested, and word spread rapidly.

Although many spoke highly of both Diane and Brad, the tone of many of those interviewed—especially Diane's former coworkers—seemed to imply that she deserved to be killed.

Mike Moran, news director at KJCT-TV in Grand Junction, where Diane had worked prior to moving to Michigan, was forthright. His comments irritated many and eventually led to his dismissal from the television station.

"If anyone could push you to the brink of doing something like that, it was her," Moran told the *Denver Post*. "We really didn't get along, and I didn't feel that badly (when I heard she was dead). She was really, really strong-willed and was constantly having personality conflicts with other people in the newsroom, including me."

Women's groups in Colorado accused him and the television station he worked for of being sexists. Leaflets were distributed at Mesa College in Grand Junction criticizing Moran and the station.

"Do career women deserve to die? Ask KJCT."

Moran didn't stop there. He also defended Brad.

"Brad was likeable, especially at first. He warmed up to people real well," Moran told the *Enquirer*. "And there was no doubt that Diane wore the pants in the family. Diane could be up-front, abrasive and pushy. Anything you could describe as a domineering person was Diane all the way."

Three days after the interviews, Moran was fired by station manager Jan Hammer.

"Mr. Moran has been dismissed because of statements previously and currently made toward Mrs. Diane King and other past statements he has made in violation of company policy," she said.

Moran later said he thought his dismissal was the "ultimate irony for our business," a news director getting fired for talking to the media.

Although definitely in the minority, Moran wasn't the only one to come forward with disparaging remarks about Diane. Several others came forward to sympathize with, if not defend, Brad.

Jerry Martin, a former cameraman at WUHQ-TV, told the *Kalamazoo Gazette* of Diane's cold-blooded quest for the news. One incident, he said, illustrated Diane's real personality. He explained that he had been grieving over the loss of his infant son when he was assigned to do a story with Diane in the same room of the hospital where his son had recently died.

"I started getting really sick so I put down the equipment and left the room," he told reporters. "She chased me down the hall and said, 'What the hell are you doing? You're going to have to shoot this.' That's the kind of heartless person she was.

"I think (Brad) had motivation (to commit the murder), but I think he was smart enough that he didn't do it. If she treated him in their private life the way she treated everybody in her professional life . . . you can only take so much."

Brad also got a boost in the media from his Grand Rapids attorney, James Brady. Realizing the impact the media could have on a jury in a small county like Calhoun, Brady decided to go on the offensive.

"He is absolutely innocent," said Brady, who had been retained by Brad several months before, to the *Grand Rapids Press*. "We don't know what happened and I don't think the police know what happened.

"They've questioned him and harrassed his family, and gone all over the country following him. They've turned members of his wife's family against him. They've done whatever they could to make his life miserable."

In an interview with the *Enquirer* a day later, Brady continued his aggressive stance toward Calhoun County authorities' handling of the investigation. Brady lashed out, furious at lawmen's inference that his client was trying to flee Colorado at the time of his arrest.

"He has no desire to run from these charges," he told the *Enquirer*. "Based on what we know, there is no evidence against him. Whoever did this is either still in the community or is long gone . . .

"They (Calhoun County authorities) don't have any evidence. He is just a scapegoat. The arrest was made because of pressure from the tabloid media. What more evidence do they have now than they had two days after the murder? They have keyed on him because they have failed in other aspects of the investigation."

Brady argued that the case was based on pure speculation, specifically when it came to the murder weapon.

"They guess it is his gun," he said. "They said that then (a few days after the murder), but it wasn't true and it's not true now. All they are doing is guessing, trying the case in the media.

"Brad doesn't know what happened other than that someone tragically took the life of his wife who he loved very much."

While the media spewed out its version of the events surrounding Brad and Diane's life, a different drama was unfolding several hundred miles away: The battle over custody of the children.

Within hours of Brad's arrest, Freida had contacted an attorney in Colorado and asked him to file a lawsuit in Denver District Court giving her permanent custody of the children.

When Freida first heard of Brad's arrest, she had little time for celebration. She and Denise, Diane's younger sister, immediately began making plans to fly to Denver to "rescue" the children.

"Freida will be overjoyed once she gets the children back," Royal Newton, Diane's stepfather, told the media. "That is all we are waiting for. She is on her way to Colorado now."

The "rescue" wouldn't be as easy as she had hoped. Brad's parents and his brother, Scott, were also on their way to Colorado. They, too, were seeking custody of the children. And Brad's friends in Denver also wanted temporary custody of the children.

The bad blood between Brad and Freida since her attempt to gain custody of the children had spread to his family and friends. They each voiced concern about

Freida's desire to take the children away from Brad "forever."

Freida was furious. It was true her focus since Diane's death had been the children, but she thought that was only normal. They were her grandchildren and she had a duty to try to protect them any way she could. In a strange way, the turmoil over the welfare of the children had helped ease the tragedy of losing her daughter. She was too concerned about her grandchildren to have time to submit to the grief caused by Diane's murder. Her mission now, as it had been since Diane's death, was to wrestle custody of the children from Brad.

After Brad's arrest, the children were placed in Denver's Family Crisis Center, and although Freida was allowed to see them, she couldn't simply take them home to Michigan as she had hoped. She would have to wait for the Colorado courts to decide who, if anybody, would take the children. It was possible the court would put the children in foster care until a permanent decision was made. She was told that could be months.

Brad also had his own ideas. Through his Colorado attorney, he informed the court that he didn't want his children placed in Freida's care. He suggested they go to his family or his friends in the Denver area.

Then another, dramatic, twist to the custody battle developed, a twist that angered Freida and frightened investigators who had spent more than a year on the case. On Thursday, Feb. 3, the day before the custody hearing, Bernard Messer, Brad's Denver attorney, made a startling announcement. He told reporters that that 3-year-old Marler had "vivid memories" of his mother's death. According to Messer, Marler had told playmates in Denver several weeks earlier that he had witnessed the murder of his mother and that his father was not the killer.

"He claims there were two assailants. Neither was his father," Messer told reporters. "He has given a rough description of the men."

Messer's statement was news to investigators. They had briefly questioned Marler a few days after Diane's murder, but the 2-year-old had provided little information. He couldn't distinguish between the killing and the emergency personnel who had responded to the scene.

Privately, investigators doubted Marler's statements and implied that his "vivid memories" were the work of a sinister father who had planted the ideas in his child's mind in a desperate attempt to clear himself of the crime, and to prevent Freida from gaining permanent custody of the children.

The investigators' beliefs were further strengthened when they heard Messer's comments that he wanted to keep the children from returning to Michigan with Freida. Messer speculated that Freida, not Brad, would be more inclined to attempt to alter the child's memories of his mother's murder.

Messer also argued that Marler could be in danger if he returned to Michigan.

"Our overriding concern is to try and keep Marler in a neutral setting," Messer said. "I question whether Michigan is a safe place for him to be if this story is true. If it is true, there are two men out there who might not want him to continue telling his account."

However, the judge didn't buy Messer's concerns. After a week of behind-the-scenes haggling, Judge Melvin Okamoto granted custody to Freida. Brad's parents, who had appeared at the hearing with an attorney, conceded the court's decision to Freida.

"We could see how this was going and figured, why spend the money on an attorney?" Mrs. Lundeen told reporters after the hearing. In court, she had only asked the judge to allow Brad and his family to have visitation privileges until Brad's trial. The judge agreed.

Mrs. Lundeen did offer one salvo before the judge's decision.

"When you have that kind of hate in your heart," she said, referring to Freida, "it shows. It consumes you."

Freida didn't care what Brad's mother said. She was ecstatic about the court's ruling. Dressed in a red sweartshirt with the names of all 12 of her grandchildren emblazoned on white hearts, she anxiously waited for the two children.

"I'm so happy," she exclaimed outside the courtroom. "This is the best Valentine's Day present I could ever have gotten."

Shortly after the hearing, a smiling and obviously happy Marler darted from social workers to the open arms of Diane's mother, who grabbed him and hugged him tightly.

"Can we go home, grandma?" he asked.

"We sure can," she said, tears welling up in her eyes as she held him as close to her chest as she could. "We sure can."

Brad had already been returned to Michigan prior to the judge's decision on the custody battle. Despite the uncertainty over his children's welfare, Brad voluntarily waived extradition and returned to Marshall on Monday, Feb. 10, in the custody of Schoder and Stadfelt.

The next day, before an overflow crowd in a small courtroom in Marshall, Brad was formally arraigned on the murder and weapons charges.

Brad, dressed in orange, wrinkled jail coveralls, remained stoic as the charges were read. He quietly answered "yes" to several questions asked by Judge Franklin Line, but didn't make any additional comments.

During the brief hearing, Brady asked the court to set a bond so that Brad could be released from custody and assist in his own defense. Despite arguments that he had local ties and had no criminal record, Line denied the request and ordered Brad held without bond.

Interestingly, Sahli suggested to Line that a gag order be imposed to prevent the case from being tried in the media. Line took the request under advisement and asked both sides to provide briefs to the court concerning the gag order.

Brady did not seem as concerned as Sahli about the adverse publicity surrounding the case.

"He's (Sahli) calling for the farmer after he let the horse out of the barn," he told reporters, implying that prosecutors and investigators had spent a year already talking to the media about the case. "Now what he is saying is the defense can't have the same access."

After the hearing, Brady continued his media barrage.

"They seem to have created the rules way back last February with their weekly, if not daily, press conferences," he said as cameras and tape recorders buzzed from the dozens of reporters clamoring for the latest quote. "They have so tainted the public that it raises the question of whether or not they can have a fair trial."

Brady also took the opportunity to proclaim his client's innocence, suggesting Brad's arrest was simply a case of a prosecutor trying to appease a clamoring media and public.

"It's been a year of unanswered questions and they let the trail get cool, and now he's a scapegoat," he told reporters.

A few days later, another hearing was held to determine whether a gag order would be imposed. It was not. Judge Line rejected Sahli's request, saying there was no substantial evidence to indicate that the defendant's right to a fair trial would be damaged by continued access to the media.

"There is only mere surmise that adverse publicity at this point will deny the defendant a fair trial, and this mere surmise is not sufficient to justify a 'gag order'," Line said.

Line ordered Brad held in the county jail without bond pending his preliminary hearing, which was scheduled for early March.

CHAPTER 15

BRAD'S PRELIMINARY HEARING at the courthouse in Marshall would not be a standard one-day affair. Because of scheduling conflicts, the four-day hearing would stretch over two weeks.

For months people in the area had anxiously awaited the proof tying Brad to Diane's death. If they were looking for a smoking gun, they were going to be disappointed. Like the investigation, the prosecution of Brad King would not be presented in a neat little package. There had been nothing quick about the investigation, and there would be nothing quick about the prosecution.

Over the next several days, Sahli and his assistants would present a variety of witnesses, friends, lovers, neighbors and coworkers. All would present significant information, but none would provide what Sahli so desperately wanted: an eyewitness or a piece of evidence that would directly and unequivocally tie Brad to the murder.

Sahli had spent most of his career as an assistant county attorney, only ascending to the top prosecutor job because his boss, Conrad Sindt, had been appointed district judge several months earlier. Although Sahli had prosecuted several successful cases in Calhoun

County, this was by far the biggest case he had ever been involved in, let alone led. The community was anxiously awaiting his performance.

On a cold March 12th morning, the city of Marshall awoke to the anticipation of Brad's hearing. The large trucks mounted with satellite dishes that surrounded the small courthouse, signaled the arrival of Brad's day in court.

The coffee shops and antique stores along Main Street bustled with the small town excitement of a major event. A quiet buzz could be heard throughout the village. It was bigger than the annual homes tour, more eagerly anticipated than the rush of tourists during the Christmas season.

And it would be the last time the city would be host to the Brad and Diane King media circus. If Brad was bound over for trial, the case would shift to the county courthouse in Battle Creek for the trial. The media and all its peripheral excitement would go along with it.

Inside the small second-floor courtroom, security was tight. Calhoun County Sheriff's deputies lined the walls, their weapons easily visible. The jury box was crammed with photographers and cameramen from local and national media outlets.

Brad was escorted to his seat at the defense table by a throng of deputies. Dressed in orange jail coveralls, he wore handcuffs and a body chain, and his ankles were shackled together.

Brad, who had refused to speak publicly since his arrest, had gained weight and let the hair on the sides of his balding head return. His appearance was soft, pudgy. Yet, there were those penetrating, glaring, blue eyes that could focus on a person for lengthy periods of time without acknowledgment. He sat smugly at the defense table as District Judge Marvin Ratner entered the courtroom.

The massive security rankled Brady. He believed his client was again the victim of unfair mass media attention. Before the hearing began, Brady asked the court to order the sheriff's department to ease its security measures.

"I object to my client's clothing and being handcuffed with a body chain and foot gear," he said, explaining that he thought the security was an overreaction to the scrutiny the department had received since the murder. "The concern I have, because of the high profile of this case, evidenced by the TV coverage that we are currently experiencing, is that it might taint the potential jurors in this county."

Brady argued that showing Brad under heavy security implied he was guilty and took away his right of presumed innocence.

"I just don't know the reasons for it," he said, shaking his head. "If Mr. King had done something to cause this concern, then I would say that he deserves to be shackled the way he is. But there isn't any evidence or any indication that he's done anything to warrant this."

The "tainting of potential jurors" became a major theme Brady espoused throughout Brad's preliminary hearing. The case had generated so much publicity in a county known more for its cereal manufacturing than its murders that Brady believed it would be virtually impossible for Brad to receive a fair trial. He would lay the groundwork for a change of venue in each and every instance he could.

Sahli, realizing there wasn't a need for the extensive security, told the court he would not object to having Brad's handcuffs and body chain removed. However, he said it was imperative to at least maintain the shackles on Brad's ankles. Judge Ratner agreed. He ordered everything but the ankle restraints removed.

Brad remained silent when the judge announced his directive. He continued to sit smugly at the defense table as the deputies removed the iron manacles. Whether because of defiance, embarrassment or fear, Brad showed little emotion. He appeared aloof, unwilling to allow those around him to see any signs of weakness.

Brady drew the ire of Diane's family when he requested that all potential witnesses be sequestered, including Diane's mother, Freida.

Sahli objected. He had told the family he would do everything he could to ensure that Freida be allowed to remain in the courtroom.

"I would ask that she be allowed to remain," Sahli told the court. "She has expressed a desire to be in the courtroom. She is the victim's mother and I would like her to be able to remain."

Freida, the backbone of Diane's clan, definitely wanted to watch the proceedings firsthand, as did others in the family. They wanted Brad to see their faces, to feel Diane's presence in the courtroom.

However, Brady was adamant in his opposition. He knew Freida would be one of the key witnesses against his client, especially if there was a trial. He didn't want her to have the opportunity to listen to everyone's theories of the case and then mold her own testimony to fit.

"I have no idea what her testimony is, but because of the animosity and the history between her and my client, I believe that it will be key testimony. Therefore, I request that she be sequestered," Brady said.

Judge Ratner agreed and banished Freida and all other witnesses from the courtroom. He also prohibited all witnesses from listening to the testimony in news reports or discussing the evidence with each other during the duration of the preliminary hearing.

That would be difficult. For months, friends and family had discussed every aspect of the case. And they weren't about to stop now. They would just have to keep the discussions among family and outside the presence of court officials or the media.

Despite the circus atmosphere surrounding the hearing, it began quietly. There were no opening statements, no announcement by Sahli of a grand design to his prosecution. As he would be throughout the prosecution of the case, Sahli was reserved and soft-spoken. He seemed awed by the enormity of the case. He spoke cautiously.

Brady was just the opposite. From the outset, it was clear what strategy he intended to use: intimidation and obstruction. He was on his feet, doggedly challenging Sahli at every possible opportunity. He believed Sahli's case to be a loosely knit compilation of circumstance and innuendo, woven together by obscure strands of evidence. He knew a tear in any one piece of evidence could doom Sahli's case. And that's what Brady intended to do—attempt to shred each and every piece of evidence that Sahli presented.

Brady strenuously objected to several aspects of Sahli's presentation in an attempt to prevent damaging testimony from being presented at the preliminary hearing or, more important, at Brad's trial, if there was to be one. Brady had another reason: anything that was said in the courtroom during the next few days would be meticulously reported in the media, especially any evidence relating to Brad's extramarital affairs.

Although Brady was confident he could keep that type of testimony from a jury at the time of a trial, he was concerned that any potential juror would already know about Brad's sexual escapades if the judge allowed the testimony to be given at the preliminary hearing and subsequently reported by the media.

He had no doubt that the media would focus on the testimony surrounding the affairs, rather than the flimsy evidence that had led to Brad's arrest.

The high-profile and complex legal issues would make it a tedious case for Judge Ratner. Throughout the preliminary hearing, Ratner would take several long recesses to research the numerous objections Brady raised.

One thing was clear from the beginning—Brady was prepared. During the first day alone, he objected dozens of times, often stymieing Sahli's attempts to elicit information from key witnesses.

The testimony at the four-day hearing came from family, friends, law enforcement officers and ballistics experts. Sahli traced the evolution of Brad and Diane's marriage from its happy beginning to its tragic end. He tried to show motive, opportunity and execution.

The first day began with the testimony of law enforcement officers and emergency personnel. But it wasn't until late afternoon, when Sahli called Freida to the stand, that the courtroom came alive.

Freida, with a clear mission in mind, walked deliberately to the witness stand to begin what she had waited months to do. She wanted to be a moving force in the conviction of her son-in-law for the murder of her daughter.

Although it was apparent that Freida had a lot to say, she wasn't going to be allowed to say it during this appearance in court. Twice during Freida's testimony, Judge Ratner took lengthy recesses to review Brady's challenges.

Brady's unrelenting objections irritated Sahli, breaking his train of thought as he attempted to question Freida about the events surrounding Diane's death.

When Freida was allowed to answer Sahli's questions, she told the story of a daughter frightened by an obsessed fan while desperately trying to save her marriage. Her testimony was anti-climatic, in part because Sahli didn't dwell on the troubled side of the marriage. Instead he concentrated on the specific events of the three days prior to the murder.

The second day of the hearing continued Sahli's methodical approach to the case and Brady's continuous objections.

Throughout the first two days, the testimony had been about procedural police work. Although there had been testimony about Brad's peculiar behavior at the scene, nothing had been as damaging or revealing as the testimony of Anne Hill, one of Brad's former lovers, on the trial's third day.

Anne didn't want to testify, but she was driven by a sense of guilt.

The attractive, dark-haired woman took the witness stand amid the murmur of dozens of observers. It was the testimony everyone in the courtroom and community had anticipated. Was this the woman for whom Brad had killed his wife? Few in the media knew what to expect. They weren't alone. For the first time in the hearing, Brad seemed on edge. He, too, was anxious to hear what Anne would say about their relationship.

Brad leaned forward in his chair as Anne hesitantly took the witness stand. She spoke softly, recounting how she and Brad met and how their relationship had evolved from student–teacher to lovers. Sahli was desperate to have her testimony included in the hearing. Brady was just as adamant that it not be allowed. He had read her statements and knew how damaging they could be.

It was Brady's job today to lay the groundwork for future motions. He would do everything he could to keep the court and the media from hearing the sordid details of Brad and Anne's sexual relationship.

Sahli knew he was walking on thin legal ground. He proceeded slowly, working up to the fall day in 1990 when the two had made love for the first time, in a park near campus.

"Can you tell us what happened at the park?" Sahli asked.

"The relationship progressed beyond being friends," Anne said, never looking at Brad. "We talked and it became a physical relationship."

"I am going to have to object to this line of questioning," Brady told Judge Ratner. "Number one, relevancy. Number two, character. This line of questioning is wholly improper. What Mr. Sahli is attempting to do is scandalize not only this court, but the entire jury pool of this county. He wants to prejudice this defendant at his trial. This is not relevant testimony. It deals specifically with character, and that is not an issue here."

Sahli was shaking his head in disagreement as Brady continued to state his objections.

"Are you introducing this evidence with regard to character?" Ratner asked Sahli.

"No, your honor," Sahli answered. "It is motive. I am not introducing it as character evidence at all."

Sahli went on to explain that Michigan case law allowed for past sexual acts to be introduced as evidence for purposes of showing or proving motive.

Brady, armed with a handful of cases outlining Michigan law, was ready to disagree.

"In terms of evidence, the prosecutor cannot introduce character evidence," he said. "And he knows it."

"Mr. Sahli said it is for motive, not character," Ratner explained, seemingly arguing Sahli's case for him.

"I'm getting to that," Brady said as he turned and walked toward the defense table where additional law books lay. "He can't put that testimony in under the umbrella of motive when there isn't any relation to motive in terms of time. What he is attempting to do here by this person's testimony is show that their relationship, these sexual acts, make him a bad person. . . . And I don't think the prosecutor can do that. . . . It just doesn't make sense to allow him to introduce it because every bad act he can ascribe to this defendant could come in under the broad brush of a motive. And there has to be more of a nexus, more of a connection between that relationship and this offense. And there isn't.

"Under Michigan law, Mr. Sahli cannot simply come in and say, 'Your honor, I'm offering this to prove motive,'" Brady argued.

"Well, there's already been testimony from Mrs. Barbara Elgutta about problems in the marriage," Sahli said. "And if Mr. Brady is so concerned about news media coverage, why did he oppose my gag order request? But I'd have no objection to the Court using its authority to take the media out of the courtroom at this time."

Ratner immediately refused Sahli's suggestion to clear the courtroom. Instead, he took a short recess to review the case law. When he returned to court, he overruled Brady's objection and allowed Sahli to pursue the questioning about the affair.

Brady was not happy. He was confident that Ratner could separate the two and would sustain his objection. However, Ratner's ruling paved the way for Sahli to get into the news coverage what he doubted would be allowed at trial: Brad's sexual escapades at WMU during the months prior to the murder.

Although there would be countless reams of testimony during the hearing, Brady knew he had lost an important battle. He now had to seriously consider asking the court for a change of venue if Brad was ordered to stand trial.

In a way, Ratner's decision could make the request for a change of venue easier. There was no doubt in Brady's mind that every story, television report and radio broadcast would lead with Anne Hill's testimony about Brad's extramarital affair.

Under gentle prodding by Sahli, Hill continued to tell of the relationship she had with Brad. She talked of his afternoon visits to her apartment, the trip to his farm and her belief that he was a single parent in the throes of a bad divorce.

She also spoke of a conversation she had with him a few weeks after the murder.

"He was upset that the investigation was focusing on him," she recalled. "He was upset they weren't looking into any other suspects. He said they were trying to pin it on him. He characterized it as a witch hunt, that Calhoun County was after him because he had been fired from a job here, that he was married to a Native American, that he said he was part Native American, and that it was all an issue of prejudice, that the Calhoun County Sheriff was very prejudiced."

She also startled courtroom observers when she testified that Brad bragged to her about his ability to shoot a .22 caliber rifle.

"He said he especially enjoyed hunting for deer with a bow and arrow because he said hunting with a rifle wasn't sporting for him," she said, recalling a conversation she had with him a few months before Diane's murder. "He said there was no skill involved because he was such a good shot he could kill a deer instantly."

By the end of the fourth day, 26 witnesses had testified. Although his battles with Brady had been an exhausting, irritating experience, Sahli felt he had presented enough evidence to force Judge Ratner to order Brad to stand trial.

Sahli's closing argument was a mechanical, fact-driven oratory. He talked about motive and opportunity. His reasons were based on specific pieces of evidence, each separate, but once pieced together they presented

a pattern that he believed led directly to Brad's involvement as the sole killer of Diane King.

"There has been testimony that Mrs. King told friends
that she and her husband were having marital problems,"
Sahli began. "I believe that's best illustrated by the fact
that the defendant on the night of the day his daughter was born was at a bar with Anne Hill when his
wife thought he was at home with her son, Marler, and
her mother. There has been testimony that Brad complained to Anne Hill about money, about his personal
life."

Sahli went on to explain how Brad had mistakenly
thought Diane was returning to their Marshall home
alone the night of her murder. He challenged early
speculation that Diane was killed by an obsessed fan,
indicating evidence he had presented at the four-day
hearing discounted that theory. He used Brad's own
statements to Schoder to dissect the stalker theory.

"Diane wouldn't get out of the car until Brad came
out and met her," he said. "Brad knew she was frightened. He knew she wouldn't get out of the car, yet he
goes for a walk and says he was gone when his wife
arrived. I think it is significant that Mrs. King was shot
outside her automobile. She had already gotten out of
her automobile."

Then Sahli moved on to the testimony surrounding the
rifle, shell casings and the bootprints found near where
the rifle was recovered from the creek.

Although Sahli had to stop short of saying positively
that the weapon recovered from the creek was the gun
that actually killed Diane, he did question the unlikely
possibility that the weapon had been in the creek for a
long time and that it had no connection to the murder.
He questioned Brad's responses about the rifle during
his statement to Schoder.

"The defendant was asked about a .22 caliber rifle,"
Sahli continued. "Detective Schoder asked if he owned

one. He said, 'I had an old one, but I sold it while I was in Colorado in 1984. I don't know who I sold it to.' Yet, three witnesses come into court and say they saw Brad with a gun that looked similar to the one used to kill Diane King.

"I think it is also interesting that on the night of Feb. 9, when Deputy Picketts approached the defendant and asked if he had any weapons, the defendant said, 'I have a shotgun in the house.' That is a strange statement to make to a police officer who approaches you and asks if you have any weapons."

One of the key elements to his case, Sahli thought, was the strangeness of Brad's actions at the scene of the murder.

"His reaction to finding his wife was also interesting," Sahli said, indicating his actions were unusual for a person who had just found his wife injured in their driveway. "He calls the operator. He asked for the police. He got the Marshall Police Department. He said, 'There's been an accident. My wife is hurt.' If in fact there had been an accident, his wife was hurt and he didn't have any idea why she was lying on the ground outside her car with blood coming from her mouth, why didn't he call for an ambulance? He did not give any first aid or attempt to aid his wife. He left his children in the car. He never asked to get the children out of the car until after his wife had been removed from the scene. He never asked how his wife was. He didn't ask to go with his wife. He didn't ask to follow his wife.

"Judge, this was not some unknown person that shot Diane King . . . An unknown person would not have known when Diane King was coming home. The defendant didn't even know until he got the call at 4:30. An unknown person wouldn't have taken the path (that the tracking dog followed behind the house). You recall Deputy Picketts' testimony was that he had lived on this property and said the path through the swamp would have to have been taken by someone that knew the property."

Sahli repeatedly accused Brad of lying to Schoder during the two interviews. He questioned why Brad seemed confused about whether he heard shots at or near his house the day Diane was killed.

He then turned his attention to a possible motive in the killing of Diane King.

"Mr. King was having a sexual relationship with Anne Hill. He was not happy with his wife. He told Ms. Hill that he and his wife were separated, that they were getting a divorce, that he had temporary custody of his son . . . We have a Feb. 21st conversation between the defendant and Anne Hill. The defendant says, 'Have the police talked to you yet?' She says, 'No.' He says, 'That's good. I don't want them to. I'm not telling them about you.'

"I would also finally ask you to consider the location and angle of the shot to the abdominal area of Mrs. King. I believe that the location of the shot is very significant. I believe that goes psychologically at least towards proving that the defendant was the perpetrator of this crime."

Unlike Sahli, the dynamic, middle-aged Brady was brash and argumentative. He presented his version of the events with energy and conviction. He chided the state's investigation of the case.

"After listening for these many days to the prosecutor's case," he said, rising forcefully from his chair to challenge Sahli's case, "it's substantially and significantly the same as it was in March of 1991. It didn't hold water then and it doesn't hold water now. By the prosecutor's own admission, this case is circumstantial at best.

"What's interesting about this case is that circumstantial evidence could lead a person to a point at which he can infer a fact for a factual setting from that circumstance, not force the person to make an inference, upon an inference, upon inference. And that is basically what the prosecution's whole case is here—inference."

Brady paced the floor as he analyzed and criticized the state's case, witness by witness. He questioned Sahli's focus on the fact that Brad had initially called the police instead of calling for an ambulance when he found his wife lying in the driveway.

"Let's talk a little bit about Mr. King's supposed— I don't know—suspicious conduct from the point of calling the Marshall dispatch," Brady said. "Interesting. He finds his wife wounded or stricken down by an accident. He goes and he calls the police. A man, a husband and a father in search of aid got the operator looking for assistance . . . It's interesting that Mr. Sahli completely chose to ignore the dispatcher's description of Mr. King's demeanor over the phone. The dispatcher's testimony was that Mr. King was distraught. He was emotional . . .

"And then there is this suspicious conduct in terms of Mr. King not going and getting involved with the emergency people. One little thing that seems to be forgotten is that Mr. King was ordered, I repeat, ordered to stay near the house by Deputy Picketts. And during that time, he was subject to long questioning by at least one and maybe two deputies. And it was at the time his wife was removed that he was then allowed to get the children . . . There was direct testimony that he made an attempt to approach (the location where his wife and children were) and he was ordered away. Everything he did is being held against him in terms of that scene . . . I am not an expert, but I assume every human being might react differently in a situation like that."

Brady continued to dissect testimony, especially when it came to the rifle.

"In terms of the weapon, one thing is clear: this weapon cannot be identified as the murder weapon. You heard Detective Sergeant Cilwa. The question I asked was very simply, do you have an opinion based on any scientific certainty that this can be the weapon? He couldn't do that. It could have been the murder weapon, but no one can say with scientific certainty that it was.

"In terms of the two bullets retrieved from Mrs. King's body, it's interesting that the (state's expert) couldn't, with any certainty, tie those bullets to the weapon or to each other . . . He couldn't say with any certainty that those two bullets even came from the same weapon, let alone from the rifle they recovered . . . He said the fact is that the .22 caliber bullets (removed from her body) could have easily been fired from a pistol as well as any other .22 caliber rifle."

Brady chided the state for being unable to specifically tie the rifle to Brad. Although three people had testified that they had seen a rifle similar to that at Brad's house, Brady said, only 15-year-old Christopher Sly was confident enough to say that that was the weapon. And when he did identify it, he did it through photographs supplied by the detectives.

"He said, 'That looks like the gun,' " Brady said. "He never touched it. He never felt it. He never came up to it . . . And when you take the fact that this child never came forward with this information until nine months after the murder, his testimony becomes a little bit clouded, and perhaps in doubt. Especially when the child says, 'I know this is a .22 because this is like my dad's .22.' And then his dad testifies and says, 'No way. My .22 is not even at all similar to this weapon.' "

Brady went on to discount several other pieces of evidence, including the bootprints found near the weapon. He said the print was that of a very common brand of boot that hundreds of people in Michigan wore regularly.

"I think the testimony proves a point that that type of sorrel boot or outdoor boot, L. L. Bean, is a common brand. The bootprint proves nothing."

Brady also challenged Freida's testimony, especially her comments that Diane wanted the children to stay with her, rather than return home to Marshall. As he had done when she was on the witness stand, Brady questioned why Diane would want to leave Kateri with her mother while she was still breast-feeding the infant.

"So this thing that Mrs. Freida Newton testified about is unbelievable," he said. "And it makes her entire testimony not credible."

Brady spent several minutes discussing Brad's relationship with Anne Hill, the only coed called by the state to testify about Brad's affairs during the months prior to Diane's murder.

According to Brady's theory, Brad and Hill hadn't had any sexual relations since mid-December, almost two months prior to Diane's death.

"Whatever that was, it was over on the 19th of December," Brady said. "So if that was the motive, it was gone."

He also questioned why Brad would resort to murder because of alleged marital problems.

"Is that a motive for murder?" Brady asked rhetorically. "I think the testimony concerning the marital infidelities was offered not for a motive, but to smear the character of Brad King.

"I just think, your Honor, in terms of this evidence that we've heard, specifically, in terms of a lack of any relation between what they believe the murder weapon to be and this defendant, there is insufficient evidence to bind this defendant over for trial.

"There has to be some evidence. This is the most serious crime we have in the state. This evidence is circumstantial. Mr. Sahli is requesting this Court to simply bind this case over for trial on mere and pure speculation."

At the end of Brady's argument, Brad lowered his head into his hands. Brad, like his attorneys, didn't expect the charges to be dismissed at the preliminary hearing. Since his arrest several weeks before, he had known his case was going to trial.

However, Diane's family didn't know what to expect. When Ratner took almost a two-hour recess to review notes of the four-day hearing, they panicked. As time passed, the family became more frantic. They roamed the halls of the courthouse, searching for any information that could ease their worries.

By the time Judge Ratner returned to the courtroom, they were in an emotional frenzy.

"I want to apologize for my tardiness, but I wanted to give as much consideration as possible to this matter," Ratner said, his opening remarks doing little to encourage Diane's family. "It's obvious it is an unusual case.

"The purpose of a preliminary examination is to find whether a crime has been committed. And after making that finding, to determine whether there is probable cause to believe that the defendant committed the crime.

"We must remember that this is a probable cause hearing. If the case goes to Circuit Court for a trial, the standard is beyond reasonable doubt, which is a higher and more difficult standard.

"It is clear that a murder has been committed. The difficult question confronting the court is who committed the crime . . . No eyewitnesses testified concerning who fired the fatal bullet. Instead, the Court has been presented with a series of circumstances which the People contend clearly connect the defendant to the crime."

Ratner cited several pieces of circumstantial evidence that seemed to tie Brad to the murder of his wife, including the fact that he and the children were the only other people in the area at the time of the murder. He discussed the location of the shell casing in the barn loft and the ballistics expert's testimony that the shell casing in the loft had been fired by the rifle found in the creek. Also, he mentioned the use of the tracking dog and its discovery of a "track."

"There are circumstance upon circumstance which confirm each other," he added. "Taken all together, these circumstances are compelling and convincing and pass the threshold of probable cause.

"Certainly the testimony of the defendant's marital difficulties with the victim as well as his extramarital affairs give credence to a probable motive.

"In addition, the circumstances surrounding the homicide establish premeditation. The evidence, as far as this Court is concerned, clearly indicates the defendant lay in wait for the victim and fired more than one shot to accomplish his purpose.

"Based upon these findings, the defendant is bound over for trial. He is remanded to the Calhoun County Jail without bond."

Brad remained stoic. He talked briefly to his attorney and was then led out of the courtroom, back downstairs to his cell.

Across the courtroom, Diane's family was ecstatic. It was the first step. It had been difficult, but it was worth it, Freida told reporters outside the courtroom.

Also outside, a smiling but quiet Sahli would only admit that "No case is easy." He refused further comment as he left the building.

Brady was disappointed but not without hope.

"Probable cause is a pretty low standard," he said. "Their evidence is slight to exaggerated."

He also informed reporters that he thought he had an

excellent chance at getting the trial moved from Calhoun County.

"Do you think he can get a fair trial?" he asked rhetorically.

CHAPTER 16

August 1992

TWO PEOPLE WERE distinctly unhappy: Brad King and James Brady. Brad wanted out of jail and Brady wanted to be paid. Both desires had little chance of being fulfilled.

In a surprise move that even caught his attorneys off guard, Brad rose from the defense table during a pre-trial hearing Aug. 11 and spoke publicly for the first time about his arrest and the fact that bond had not been set in his case.

"I did not kill my wife," he told the hushed courtroom. "And I want to be released from jail so I can show this county that I did not kill my wife."

Dressed in the standard orange jail coveralls and slippers, Brad stood defiantly in the extremely small courtroom on the first floor of the Battle Creek courthouse as Circuit Court Judge Conrad Sindt and other court personnel watched in disbelief.

"I've spent over six months in jail, and I'm an innocent man," he said, as his attorneys quietly looked on. "I feel I'm unjustly charged and that it's a political issue with Mr. Sahli . . . The fact that I've been in jail for six months is ridiculous."

Sindt listened to Brad's statement but gave no indication that he would grant his request to set bond. The past six months had been brutal for Brad. His days spent in a six-man cell at the county jail in Marshall were tediously slow. He was occasionally allowed to see his son, Marler, but only under strict, supervised conditions. His cellmates were the type of people he had arrested as a Pontiac police officer and later corralled as a Calhoun County probation officer. Brad wanted out of jail and out of their presence. He told anyone who would listen that he didn't belong there.

However, he had little chance of being released. He had been held without bond since his arrest in January 1992, and no motion had been filed by Brady seeking release. That angered Brad even more. For the past several weeks, Brad and Brady had disagreed on several issues, including how the case was being moved through the legal system and what strategies were to be used at the trial.

But the real threat to Brady's continued representation of Brad centered on whether or not Brad could come up with enough money to pay for his services. Brad's mother had already spent thousands of dollars on his defense, and the question now was whether she intended to spend any more. Brad was broke. It was up to his family to decide whether they would retain Brady, seek another attorney, or have Brad declare himself indigent and ask the court to appoint a lawyer to represent him.

Brad was also concerned that Brady, whose main office was across the state in Grand Rapids, wasn't spending enough time on his case. That opinion was not discouraged by Brady's co-counsel, Battle Creek lawyer Virginia Cairns.

Brady's problems with Brad became public during a hearing before District Judge Sindt in late July.

Sindt, a former prosecutor and Sahli's boss for several years, was assigned the King murder case shortly after Brad had been ordered to stand trial in March. Sindt, a meticulous man who liked to keep his court docket up to date, had worked hard to clear his calender for what everyone expected to be a trial lasting six weeks to two months. Sahli had already hinted to his former boss that he expected to call approximately 100 witnesses. The trial was set for Sept. 1, but that now seemed doubtful.

In a discussion in Sindt's small chambers in the back of the Battle Creek courthouse, Brady told Sindt that unless some arrangements could be made for him to be paid, he was out of the case. Brady said Brad's family had been unable or unwilling to come up with the money needed for a lengthy trial.

Sindt was concerned. Brady's departure would force additional delays as a new attorney was found. He could appoint Cairns to handle the case, but he was reluctant to do so. Although she was a courthouse regular in Calhoun County, Sindt thought she lacked the experience necessary to handle a case of this magnitude.

One possible option was to find another attorney who could lead the case, please Brad and get along with Cairns.

At the Aug. 11 hearing, Brady seemed to have worked out his problems with Brad. He earnestly argued a motion for a change of venue, citing the results of a survey conducted by a company retained by the defense.

According to the survey, more than 36 newspapers in the region had run stories about the case, including more than 60 articles in the *Battle Creek Enquirer*, the *Marshall Chronicle* and the *Kalamazoo Gazette*. Of the 200 potential jurors surveyed in Calhoun County, 94 percent had knowledge of the case, 36 percent believed Brad was responsible for Diane's death and 27 percent believed he was guilty.

Despite the apparent overwhelming knowledge about the case in the community, Sindt denied Brady's motion. He told Brady he wanted to attempt to impanel a jury before making the drastic move to change venues.

"I think we should wait until we have found out if it is impossible to do it here," he said.

Brady disagreed with Sindt's ruling, telling reporters after the hearing that he thought it would be unlikely that an impartial jury could be found in Calhoun County.

Brady never got the chance to find out whether Brad King could get a fair trial in Calhoun County. What Sindt had dreaded for weeks came true on Aug. 27 when Brad issued a press release indicating he had fired Brady.

"I have initiated this change due to actions on the part of James Brady that have resulted in the breakdown of the attorney-client relationship," Brad said in a one-page release issued from the county jail. "I have lost confidence in his ability to defend me."

Brad also said he had retained Cairns and added another local attorney, John Sims, to lead his defense. The family, after several discussions with Cairns and others in the legal community, had chosen the 40-year-old Sims. Whatever their financial problems had been with Brady, they were able to reach an agreement with Sims.

Sims, a lifelong resident of Calhoun County, immediately made his presence known. In conjunction with Cairns, he filed several motions aimed at overturning the momentum that he believed prosecutors had gained during the months since Brad's arrest.

He clearly had a different defense strategy than that employed by Brady. Where Brady was more of a legal technician, Sims seemed interested in using his charm to win. Although a competent legal strategist, he did not have the abrasive, razor's-edge approach that Brady had used at the preliminary hearing.

One of the first things Sims did was ask Sindt to set bond for Brad, a move that delighted Brad and his family.

"Murder is bailable in this state," Sims argued to the

court, indicating it was unfair to keep Brad in custody without the opportunity for bond, especially as Brad had indicated no desire to flee. "He's committed to staying here and fighting these charges," Sims said.

Sims suggested that a $50,000 bond would be reasonable. Sahli countered that he didn't want any bond set, but if Sindt were inclined to do it, he thought $1 million would be appropriate.

Sims also started a widespread offensive, including attacks on the prosecution's version of the murder, the sheriff department's handling of the investigation and the irresponsibility of the media's coverage of the case.

Sims asked Sindt to bar reporters from attending the pre-trial hearings, saying the coverage had been inaccurate and unfair to his client. He even asked the court to dismiss the charges.

"This case is built on inference upon inference, and there were no facts to support those inferences," he wrote in a motion filed shortly after he took over the case. "There is suspicion, conjecture, possibilities and a great deal of hope by the prosecutors, but no factual evidence."

Although Sindt denied most of the defense's requests, including dismissing the charges, he did set a bond for Brad: $750,000.

In addition to the bond, which would require someone to post $75,000 in cash, Sindt placed several restrictions on Brad's release. Brad could not leave Calhoun County. He had to give the court his address, be placed in the custody of his minister, give up his driver's license and remain inside his residence from 6 P.M. to 7 A.M.

Brad and his attorneys, family and friends were ecstatic with Sindt's decision. They hoped Brad would soon be released from custody, a situation that correspondingly angered and scared people who were scheduled to testify against him.

Unfortunately for Brad, Sindt's decision to set bond

didn't immediately clear the way for his release. Although family and friends were working diligently to secure his freedom, there were problems, mainly with finding him a place to live. Because he'd moved after the murder, he'd given up his rented farmhouse several month prior to his arrest. Many landlords in Battle Creek and the surrounding area rejected requests to allow Brad to move into one of their apartments.

One landlord agreed to rent an apartment, but changed his mind when he found out through media reports that the person who wanted the apartment was Brad.

"How would you like to have him living next door to you?" said one resident, when asked by reporters how she would feel about having him as a neighbor during the trial. "You wouldn't know what to expect. He's charged with murder," she said.

Randy Wright, Brad's close friend and confidant who had stood beside him since his arrest, was angered by the difficulty of finding a suitable place for Brad to live. He chastised the community, saying it was imperative for Brad to be released from custody so that he could assist in his own defense.

"The psychological impact of his being in jail is devastating," Wright told reporters.

Others were not so enthusiastic about Brad's release.

"He might as well get used to it," said one friend of Diane's. "If I have my way, that's where he's going to spend the rest of his life."

CHAPTER 17

ON THE EVE of his trial, Brad decided to talk. Not to prosecutors, but to the local newspaper. Irritated over his inability to gain release on bond, Brad decided to tell his side of the story.

Two days before he was to stand trial for first degree, premeditated murder, Brad granted a jailhouse interview to Trace Christenson, a reporter for the *Battle Creek Enquirer*. It was the first and only interview Brad would grant.

Christenson, a 40ish man who had spent years as a cops and crime reporter, sat anxiously in Virginia Cairns' stark second-floor law office across from the courthouse in Battle Creek. Brad, who remained in the county jail in Marshall, would speak to him by telephone with Cairns listening in. Cairns demanded control. She monitored every question, scrutinized every answer.

Christenson didn't like Cairns' restraints but attempted to work his way through the situation with savvy and determination. At least he had an interview with Brad King, and no one else would have it. Despite the numerous requests from national television programs, newspapers and radio, Brad had chosen him. Christenson didn't know why and he didn't care. It was something he had been working on for months. He wasn't going to let Cairns ruin it.

However, the interview revealed nothing new about the case—only Brad's angry and emotional reaction to it, and his belief that he would be vindicated. During the telephone interview Brad discussed a wide range of subjects. At times, he seemed to be reading from a prepared script. He talked about longing for his freedom, about his love for his children, his belief in God and his longing for Diane. His emotions varied with each subject. He could be pleasant and agreeable, or arrogant and angry.

"I am right and right always wins," Brad said. "I am not guilty, and I am waiting for this to pass."

The possibility of being tried by a jury comprised of Calhoun County residents was clearly on Brad's mind.

"Get a fair trial?" he said, responding to a question. "I have my doubts about that because of the publicity that has been given this case for the past year-and-a-half. I have every confidence in my lawyers, but given what has been going on in this county in regards to this trial, that makes me nervous.

"I miss my children a lot and look at their pictures every day," he said. "That is what I think about. I also think about going back to Denver. I have a job there working with a consulting firm."

He talked about a recent supervised visit he had with Marler at the Battle Creek courthouse, saying he believed the boy had been told by Diane's relatives that he was dead. The meeting, the first between Brad and Marler since his arrest in Denver, was arranged by Sims. In exchange for the face-to-face meeting, Sims indicated he wouldn't call the 4-year-old boy to the witness stand. The meeting between father and son didn't go well. Brad was not allowed to touch Marler, and the meeting did little to raise Brad's spirits. It was obvious that Marler had changed. He didn't want to even see his father. Brad attributed that to "brainwashing" by Freida.

"He was very confused," Brad said of Marler. "It's going to require a lot of help for him to deal with death and why his father was taken away from him and why he was lied to about it."

Many in the legal community thought the interview was a clear sign that Brad would not take the witness stand at his trial. Court observers saw it as an attempt by the defense to get the "human side" of their client to the public without the risk of a cross-examination.

As usual, Sahli declined to comment on the facts of the case, or on Brad's statements to the *Enquirer*. Whether Sahli was trying to avoid any legal problems, or simply had an aversion to the media, he remained unapproachable.

The community was not impressed with Brad King's comments to the *Enquirer*. After the preliminary hearing, most residents of Calhoun County had concluded that Brad was Diane's killer.

He did little to erase that belief in the interview which was displayed on the top front page of the *Enquirer*'s Sunday edition. In fact, it might have hurt his attempt to be released from jail prior to the trial. Although friends and family had raised the $75,000, which was 10 percent of his $750,000 bond, they still couldn't find a place for him to live. No one wanted Brad King living near them.

Initially, friends and relatives had found Brad an apartment to rent in Battle Creek, and they had acquired enough money to pay the first two months' rent. However, when residents of the complex found out through the media that Brad was going to move in, they rebelled. The furor caused by the tenants prevented Brad's supporters from renting an apartment. He remained in jail as the search for a place to live continued.

Meanwhile, the focus of the Diane King murder case had shifted dramatically. Speculation about who had killed Diane still circulated, but most residents passed it off as passe rumors. The overriding question now was not who killed Diane King, but could authorities prove Brad did it?

Sahli and Schoder seemed to be as much on trial as Brad. Were Schoder and his counterparts at the sheriff's department as incompetent as many Calhoun County residents had suggested during the months that the investigation dragged on? Or did Sahli's fear of losing the case make him overly cautious in waiting so long to prosecute Brad as others in the community believed?

Those were the questions on everyone's mind as the tedious process of selecting a jury began in the large, airy courtroom on the first floor of the Hall of Justice, commonly referred to as the Battle Creek courthouse.

The concerns of the community couldn't have been demonstrated any more clearly than in the county-wide elections that were conducted on the day jury selection began.

Sheriff Jon Olson, the Calhoun County sheriff for 14 years, was handily defeated. Although friends and supporters quickly moved to discount speculation that his loss was an indication that voters had lost confidence in his department, many political observers admitted privately that the Brad King murder case had played an important role in diminishing Olson's longtime popularity.

Although Sahli was unopposed in his reelection bid, the mood in the community wasn't lost on him. He appeared anxious. He rarely spoke to anyone but his staff as he walked the narrow halls between Sindt's office and the courtroom. When court wasn't in session, he often retreated to his office across the street for strategy sessions and relaxation.

Sims, on the other hand was effervescent. He combined the seriousness of the moment with the humor of a person confident in his own abilities. It was the biggest trial of his career, but that didn't stop him from enjoying it. His confidence was born of hard work and preparation.

"If I get the right (legal) decisions, I can win this thing," he quietly told a couple of peers in the hallway outside earshot of the dozens of reporters who hung on every word.

The decisions. That's what worried Sims. Despite his intense preparation, he knew that if Judge Sindt allowed Sahli to introduce certain testimony to the jury it would badly handicap his case. If Sindt agreed with Sims and refused to allow key testimony, especially that involving Brad's sexual affairs with the coeds, then he had a fighting chance.

However, those decisions would have to wait. Sindt had denied Sims' earlier request to argue the motions prior to seating a jury. Instead, the judge ordered the jury to be impaneled and then he would hear arguments on the motions outside the jury's presence.

Right now, though, Sims' first concern was that of selecting a jury. He had his doubts. His motion for a change of venue was still pending, and he thought there was a good chance the trial would be delayed several weeks because they couldn't seat a jury.

Over the next three days, people from all walks of life would come face-to-face with the man accused of murder in a case that had practically held the community hostage for more than a year. The potential jurors' actions were interesting. When the name of a potential juror was called from the more than 200 that had jammed into the courtroom, that person would be escorted into the small jury room adjacent to the courtroom.

Each juror was questioned individually to prevent the entire jury panel from being tainted. It was the first time many of the prospective jurors had ever been in a courtroom, let alone within reach of a man accused of killing his wife. It was a study in human nature.

Some would immediately look at Brad. Others never did. Some seemed honored to be the recipient of such attention, offering opinions on the legal system, rights of the accused and the philosophical question of innocence. Others attempted to shun the lawyers' scrutiny with terse, one-sentence answers designed to hasten their exit.

Throughout it all, Brad sat quietly next to Sims and Cairns. Sahli and his assistant prosecutor, Nancy Mullett, sat in wooden chairs only a few feet away. Armed guards stood nearby.

Dressed in a gray suit and tie, Brad would occasionally speak to his attorneys, but most of the time he sat passively as his blue eyes scrutinized the faces of the potential jurors.

"I think he's guilty," several responded to questions from attorneys about their knowledge of the case. Others would not be so direct.

"From what I've heard, it appears that he committed the crime, but I think I can be objective. I can listen to the evidence and then make my decision."

Another added: "I think everyone is innocent until proven guilty. But I think he is guilty."

Although every person questioned had heard about the murder and Brad's arrest, the process did not take as long as court officials had anticipated. Within three days the 12 jurors and two alternates had been chosen. There would be no need for a change of venue. Both attorneys seemed confident that they had found jurors that would listen objectively to the evidence presented at trial.

"It's as good as it's going to get," Sims said.

With the jury impaneled, Sindt had overcome one giant obstacle—a possible change of venue. Now, he was faced with a second hurdle: trying to make proper rulings out of the complex legal issues in the case. Everyone, including Brad, appeared anxious for the trial to begin.

Sindt was faced with a prosecutor who needed every piece of evidence to build his circumstantial case and a defense attorney whose main goal was to prevent prosecutors from parading an endless number of witnesses to the stand who had no bearing on the real issue of the case: who killed Diane King.

For Sims and Sahli, the arguments prior to testimony beginning probably were as important to their cases as any actual testimony would be.

After two days of skirmishing, the judge issued several rulings. To many observers, it looked as if Sims had won the battle. One of the key rulings was the testimony of the coeds about their affairs with Brad. Sims was adamant that it not be allowed.

"I have very serious problems with that kind of testimony to prove my client's guilt," Sims argued. "I don't know how it establishes that my client committed the murder. The harm here is that it paints Brad as a bad person. The jury will think: If he committed these bad acts (of adultery), why couldn't he commit other bad acts—like murder. It's unfair and it's prejudicial."

Sahli disagreed, saying the coeds' testimony illustrated "a possible motive in the case."

Sindt, after lengthy trips to the law books, accepted Sims argument. He would not allow testimony regarding Brad's sexual involvement with the coeds. However, Sahli could present testimony from the coeds detailing the lies Brad told them about his marital relationship, his military background and his Indian heritage.

"I'm not going to allow testimony about the sexual acts or relationships to be admitted until proper foundation has been laid," he said.

Sahli was livid. He thought testimony concerning Brad's infidelities with the students was clearly admissable and was important to show a motive for the killing. Sims disagreed, saying the only reason Sahli wanted to introduce that testimony was to destroy Brad's character.

Sims made it clear he didn't intend to make Brad's character an issue in the trial. And if he wasn't going to open the door to this issue, then Sahli couldn't walk through on his own, Sims argued.

Sindt also ruled, to Sahli's chagrin, that statements Diane King had made to friends and relatives about her marriage and possible divorce, her finances, the decision to quit her job and the security precautions she took after she received the threatening letter would not be allowed.

"It's like allowing Diane King to testify," Sims had argued, regarding letting the witnesses testify about what Diane had told them. "It's wrong. She's not here. I can't cross-examine her."

Sindt agreed.

"Clearly, the court finds that the personal observations of Diane King's behavior are admissable," he said. "But her statements to others about her habits and routine are clearly hearsay. If they saw her do it, they can testify about that. But they can't testify about what Diane King told them she did. That is clearly hearsay."

Again the prosecution disagreed. They argued that the statements she made to friends and relatives gave a clear picture of what was happening around the King household in the months prior to the murder. It was an exception to the hearsay rule, prosecutors said, and they wanted to use it to show Diane's state of mind.

"It's all interrelated," Sahli argued.

"It's a fairy tale," Sims shot back.

While Sims was happy with several of Sindt's decisions, he was furious about another development: a new witness. In a surprise move, Sahli asked Sindt to allow him to endorse another witness. It was Ricky McClain, a recent cellmate of Brad's who, Sahli said, would testify that Brad made statements to McClain while they were both in custody that "could be construed as guilt."

Sims was beside himself. He didn't believe the inmate, a long-time loser who was a regular visitor to the county lockup.

"He's a singing jailbird who is going to come in here and lie for his own benefit," Sims argued.

Sims knew Bradford King wasn't stupid. Brad had been in law enforcement long enough to know that the last thing you wanted to do was discuss your own case with another cellmate. There had always been and always would be cellmates seeking an opportunity to shave time off their sentences by "rolling over" on another, more important character in jail.

Sims argued that allowing McClain's testimony at this late date was prejudicial. It didn't allow him enough time to research his testimony. He argued that if prosecutors had wanted McClain to testify, they should have endorsed him several weeks before instead of springing it on the defense the day before testimony was to begin.

"Judge, we didn't learn of his testimony until Friday," Sahli said, indicating the late endorsement wasn't a planned attempt to circumvent the defense's strategy in the case. "We came forward as soon as we learned about it."

After a lengthy debate, Sindt allowed Sahli to call McClain to testify, but ordered prosecutors to immediately hand over to the defense each and every statement McClain had given to them concerning the jailhouse conversations.

"He's going to come in here and lie, that's all he is going to do," Sims argued in vain.

"I have made my decision," Sindt told Sims as the court recessed for the day. "We will see you gentlemen Thursday morning."

CHAPTER 18

FINALLY, BRAD'S DAY in court had arrived.

Screenwriters, television producers, authors and journalists from a dozen different outlets mingled in the narrow hallway outside the large courtroom on the first floor of the courthouse. The hallway and adjacent foyer would become the meeting ground for the milieu that would follow the trial for the next two months.

In a tiny room next to the courtroom, Diane's family kept a constant vigil. Pictures of Diane and her children were always present. A dream catcher, a Native American traditional object designed to ward off evil spirits, waved briskly in the window as light snow fell softly on the concrete pavement outside.

The "witness room" was off-limits to journalists, so many of the reporters mingled just outside the door, not wanting to miss anything Diane's family might say or do. Occasionally, members of the family, especially Diane's stepfather, Royal Newton, and her brother, Allen, would come into the foyer to smoke cigarettes and discuss the day's events with journalists. Freida rarely left the room. She was constantly insulated from journalists by family and friends.

The small courthouse, a renovated post office, was a maze of narrow hallways and offices. Each day, Brad would be escorted from a small holding cell, down a corridor lined with newsmen and spectators and into the expansive courtroom that seemed to dwarf the rest of the building.

For the next two months, the case would captivate Calhoun County and much of the nation. For the first time, the entire community could watch a murder trial from their own homes.

Court TV, a national cable network designed to broadcast live courtroom action across the nation, selected the King trial as its premier case. In addition to covering the trial live, Court TV also had "guest experts" in New York who critiqued the lawyers and witnesses. The result was almost like a halftime analysis on Sunday's professional football telecasts. Court TV also had call-in shows, usually during the one-hour noon recess, in which people watching on television could call with their comments.

Bars and restaurants like The Hunt Club and The Finish Line in Battle Creek turned their televisions from ESPN and other sports events to the Court TV channel. The trial was on the minds and lips of everyone. It was an important event. It had to be, it was on national television.

Attorneys on both sides also had people watching Court TV and listening to the experts' critiques to gauge how they were doing.

Kristin Jeanette-Meyers, a Court TV reporter whose broadcasts from the steps of the Hall of Justice in Battle Creek were beamed live across the country, became a celebrity during the trial. She was showered with dinner invitations and was even given a dozen roses by one of the detectives involved in the case. Everywhere she went, Meyers was bombarded with autograph requests.

Ironically, Court TV's presence altered the courtroom. It wasn't a haven for curious onlookers. It became a working office for reporters and broadcasters. Unlike other high-profile cases in Battle Creek, only a handful of court observers attended the trial. Instead of traipsing to the courthouse every day and waiting in line to get into the courtroom, most people simply stayed at home and watched the entire proceedings on television in the comfort of their own living rooms.

Even those inside the Calhoun County jail watched the case unfold on television. Every night Brad would return to his cell knowing that most of the inmates had watched every detail of the trial.

Judge Sindt gaveled the courtroom to order shortly before 9 A.M. on Nov. 12, almost 22 months after Diane was killed in the driveway of her rural home.

The jury sat passively while Sindt gave them initial instructions. They anxiously shuffled in their seats when Sindt ended his opening comments and asked the prosecution if they were ready to begin opening statements.

"Yes, your honor," Sahli said, rising from his chair. "The people are ready to proceed."

The 45-year-old Sahli had spent most of his career as a Calhoun County prosecutor. He had a lot to prove and he knew it. Before he began his case, he and his assistants set up massive time charts and graphs illustrating the various telephone calls and clandestine meetings Brad conducted with several female students during the weeks prior to Diane's murder.

"They clearly illustrate the scheme of things to come," Sahli had told reporters prior to the trial.

Sahli was nervous. He cleared his throat. He clutched the sides of the wooden podium. For months the small, ruddy-faced man had been at the center of a heated debate over the handling of the investigation and the arrest. He had maintained his silence throughout most of the community's speculation and quarreling.

Now it was his turn to prove to them that he was a capable prosecutor and not just someone who had been at the right place at the right time—Conrad Sindt's top assistant when he was selected to be a circuit court judge.

It was clear from the charts lining the front of the courtroom that this murder case wasn't going to be won or lost with the penetrating examination of one witness. There would be no smoking gun, no tearful confession in the courtroom. If Sahli was to win this case, he would have to use the same cool, clear-headedness that Diane's murderer had used when he systematically executed her in her driveway.

Sahli's opening statement was calculated and methodical. He did not shout or pace. He was not attempting to elicit excitement or anger from the jurors. He needed an attentive jury, more interested in digesting the hundreds of minute facts than being entertained.

His opening statement wasn't theatrical. It was pedestrian at best. With clear understatement, Sahli attempted to walk the jury through the days and months leading to Diane's murder.

He reconstructed the state's evidence against Brad. He used the charts and graphs to illustrate the meanderings of a philandering husband. Although he was prohibited by Sindt's rulings from describing the clandestine meetings Brad had with his students as "affairs," it was clear to everyone in the courtroom that Brad had been preoccupied with two or three students. And that preoccupation was a central element in the destruction of his marriage.

Sahli dismissed the initial speculation that Diane had been killed by a stalker. He claimed it was Brad's attempt to divert attention from the murder by creating the appearance of a stalker.

"There was no stalker," Sahli said. "Except Brad King. He is the one who made the telephone calls. He is the one who sent the letter."

Sahli told the jury he would present expert testimony indicating that in most cases where a threatening letter was sent to someone, it was usually the work of someone who knew the victim well.

"You're probably all familiar with these types of notes or letters from watching television programs and movies," he said. "In television shows and movies, these crazed killers sent these notes to the victim. But experts familiar with these types of things say they come from family members or, in some cases, the victim themselves."

In this case, we know for sure that Diane King didn't send the threatening letter. She didn't make the telephone calls, he told the jury.

At one point, almost 30 minutes into his opening statement, Sahli paused. He took a breath, then looked back at the jury.

"What do we really know about what happened on Feb. 9, 1991—the day Diane Newton King was killed," he rhetorically asked the jury, his voice rising ever so slightly. "We know what the defendant would like us to believe. We know from his two statements what he would like us to believe. We know what the inconsistencies are with what happened and with what he would like us to believe. We know what various neighbors observed that day. We know what was observed at the scene of the murder by emergency personnel and police officers. And we know what evidence was found at the scene . . . You will get to hear his two statements and then you will know that we know more than the defendant wants us to know."

Sahli, after pausing for a brief moment, then turned to an issue that he knew would crystalize in the jury's mind: the children inside the Jeep Wagoneer when Diane was gunned down.

He asked the jury to consider one question: Did Brad know the children would be with her?

If Brad was the killer, it was the one piece of evidence that no one could overlook. How could a father cold-bloodedly kill his wife in front of their two small children? Sahli thought the answer was simple: Brad didn't know they were there until after he had shot Diane.

"Mrs. Freida Newton, Diane's mother, is most emphatic that she told Brad King that Diane was on her way home," Sahli told the jury. "That's important—Diane was on her way home. It's the state's theory that the defendant didn't expect those children to be in that car."

It was clear that Sahli believed the children's presence was the one thing Brad had not prepared for; the one circumstance that essentially destroyed his plan for the perfect crime. It was the reason he had haphazardly disposed of the murder weapon in a creek bed behind the farmhouse. From the moment Brad saw the faces of his children in the backseat of the Wagoneer, his strategy had to change, Sahli told the jury. His plan was no longer perfect.

After almost 90 minutes of listening to details of the state's case, Sindt realized the jurors were tired. He decided it was time to take the morning break. The recess, midway through Sahli's opening statement, would be a harbinger of things to come. During the recess, an angry Sims complained to Sindt in his chambers that Sahli's opening statements violated the court's prior rulings.

Sims said Sahli's charts clearly listed the word "date" next to meetings Brad had with the coeds. He told Sindt he was asking for a mistrial and wanted it on the record.

When Sindt returned to the bench a few minutes later, he ordered that the jurors remain in the jury room until further notice. This scene would be repeated all too frequently during the next several weeks.

"They have violated not only the spirit, but the letter of the law," an angry Sims told Sindt. "The implication is clear. They have circumvented your ruling. I want a mistrial right now so I can go home and take a nap and forget about this mess."

Sahli, obviously shaken by the motion, defended his actions, saying he would never directly or indirectly attempt to violate the court's ruling. Almost apologetically, Sahli told Sindt he would voluntarily remove the word "date" from the charts before the jury was returned to the courtroom.

"I have not overstepped the court's ruling," he said. "I have never overstepped the court's ruling in my entire career. I don't believe I have now, and I think a mistrial is totally uncalled for."

Sims, a sarcastic smile creasing his face, turned toward the spectators, his hands stuffed into his front pockets.

"Let's take a poll, your honor," he said. "I think everyone in this courtroom knows what's going on here. If you don't think we can see through that thin veil, well . . ."

Although the trial had been in session less than a day, Sims had already asked for two mistrials.

Diane's family, unfamiliar with court strategy and proceedings, were obviously on edge as they watched the drama unfold from the second row, directly behind the prosecutor's table. With each request for a mistrial, their uneasiness grew. They feared the day they had waited for months to arrive would be erased by a defense lawyer's motion for a mistrial.

"I know he is going to get one," Diane's sister, Darlene, whispered to a person seated near her. "If he keeps at it, it's going to happen."

She was wrong. It didn't happen. At least not yet. Sindt patiently listened to Sims' angry comments, then calmly overruled the motions for a mistrial.

"I don't find those references to be so blatant as to constitute a mistrial," he said, adding that Sahli should remove the word date from the charts as he had earlier offered. "I am satisfied there has not been great damage done. Let's bring the jury back in."

Once again, Sahli returned to his methodical approach. He outlined in detail every piece of evidence the state intended to present. He discussed ballistics, the use of lasers to determine where the shots were fired from and, most important, how the shots were fired. He explained in detail the work of Travis, the tracking dog, and how important it was to the case.

And he talked of Brad's arrogance, not only at the scene, but at the funeral and during the weeks following Diane's death.

He also talked about Brad's demeanor at the murder scene, the funeral and during the weeks after the killing.

"You're going to hear the testimony of Heather Taylor, a friend of his at Western Michigan University, a student, who will tell you about a short conversation she had with the defendant on the campus of Western Michigan University two weeks after Diane King was murdered. She will tell you the defendant told her, quote: 'They don't have anything on me. They can't prove a fucking thing.' That was his statement, two weeks after the murder of his wife."

Sahli looked at his watch. He had been talking for almost two and one-half hours. He took a deep breath, appearing relieved that his opening statement was nearing the end. He walked to the front of the jury, where he stopped, facing them. For the first time, a smile crossed his face.

"Ladies and gentlemen, if the evidence comes forward as I have outlined it to you today—and I am confident the evidence is going to come across at least as I have outlined it in my opening statement, if not stronger— I am going to ask you to return a verdict of guilty of first-degree premeditated murder against Bradford King. Thank you."

Sims was ready when the court returned to session about 1:30 P.M. Unlike Sahli, Sims cherished his moments in court. He was animated, energetic.

"Bradford King is innocent," Sims enthusiastically told the jury. "There is no proof he killed his wife."

With that blanket statement, Sims opened his defense. It was his turn to discount the tremendous amount of circumstantial evidence investigators had gathered against Brad. He had to convince the jury that the charts, graphs and hundreds of hours of investigative work were not proof of Brad's guilt, but a last gasp effort by the prosecutor to create a case by overwhelming the jury with irrelevant facts to cover up a botched investigation.

"I sat through the prosecution's opening statement and thought 'Golly. We've got everything here, folks. We've got lasers, we got microwaves, we got videotapes, we got audiotapes, we got film at 11, we've got tracking dogs, we've got experts on personal behavior, we've got ballistics experts, we've got time lines, we've got slides, we've got graphs, we've got statistics, we've got everything.' Everything except something to do with why you are all here. There is only one issue in this case, folks. Who did it? There is no proof that you will see of Bradford King's guilt. Diane King is dead, but they can't prove who did it. They don't know who did it. No one will get on the witness stand and say Brad King shot her."

Sims was hyped up. He swaggered around the courtroom with the air of a street fighter stalking his opponent. He prodded the jury with rhetorical questions about the detectives' ability to investigate the crime. He argued that if Brad had killed his wife, why did it take the state so long to arrest him.

"January 31, almost a year later," he told the jury. "The testimony is going to show you that's when they decided to arrest Bradford King. That's it. Why are we here? I'll tell you why we are here—you knew I would.

"Why we are here is based upon several things, folks. No words from that witness stand are going to represent why we are here. And that is why you are going to have to listen to what is said, who says it, what they say, how they say it and what they really mean."

Sims was doing what he had to do. Sahli had spent the morning inundating the jury with a myriad of circumstantial evidence. He used massive charts to plot the murderous scheme he believed King had used to kill Diane. The numerous pieces of evidence seem unrelated at first, but when pieced together revealed a twisted, complicated murderous plot, Sahli had told the jury.

"You, as the trier of facts, are going to hear testimony from 70 witnesses and see hundreds of documents. I don't know for sure what the amount, but it's going to seem like a lot because what you see here is the power of the state against Bradford King," Sims said.

"What you are going to see is that they believe if you really want somebody bad enough you can get them, whether you've got the proof or not. As long as you have the power of the state and every law enforcement agency you can find to scour the countryside, you can get your man.

"What is this case all about?" Sims asked. "It's about insinuations, innuendo, suspicions. Not proof beyond a reasonable doubt. What you are going to hear from this witness stand is 'I believe, I thought, I think.' You are going to hear witnesses get up on that stand and say 'I know.'

"And folks, I now know, you are going to hear out and out fabricated lies. Lies! The prosecutor is going to put someone on that witness stand, at least he has listed him as a witness, that is going to lie to you," Sims said of McClain, the prisoner who had recently told authorities of an alleged conversation he had with Brad in which Brad admitted to the murder.

"That's what this case is all about," he said, showing his anger for the first time. "That's what you are going to see from this witness stand. That's what you are going to hear and that's what you are going to find. And that's all. As someone once said, you are going to hear sound and fury signifying nothing.

"There is only one issue in the case and that is who did it? And they don't know. They can't prove who did it.

"And you are going to see that. No one is going to get on this witness stand and say they saw Brad King shoot his wife. No one will get on this witness stand and say Brad King had a gun that day. No one is going to say Brad King held the gun that day and pulled the trigger that day. Nobody is going to say that. Nobody!

"You are going to hear a police officer get up here and tell you Bradford King only denied killing Diane King 27 times. The detective will say that is a soft denial."

Sims paced in front of the jury. His anger had dissipated as quickly as it had surfaced. He smiled occasionally. He was user-friendly, not stiff and mechanical as Sahli had been during his opening statement.

"What are they really doing, folks?" Sims asked rhetorically of the jury, a smile again creasing his face. "What is the proof really going to show you? It is going to show you that they are attacking a man to defend their own phoney baloney jobs. How many times have you already heard from the prosecutor that they didn't do this and they didn't do that? They've got to explain why they didn't do their jobs properly.

"And they've got to find a patsy for the mistakes they made. Well, they found one, there he is," Sims said, pointing to Brad, who intensely, but passively, listened to the comments.

Sims walked back toward the jury. He stopped, his hands thrust into the front pockets of his trousers as he contemplated his next comment. He stared at the jury. He shrugged his shoulders.

"I'm going to disappoint you because I am not going to ramble on for four hours," he said, turning his back to the jury as he sarcastically jabbed Sahli's marathon opening statement. "I don't have to. I've told you what the facts are.

"I am going to point out to you a couple of things to look for in the testimony. A few things came to mind as I listened to the prosecutor tell you about the overwhelming depth of evidence they have.

"You are going to hear that Detective Schoder took those boots from Bradford King the night of the murder," Sims said, strongly emphasizing his words. "But that's not what happened. What you are going to find out is that Bradford King offered the detectives the boots. 'You want boots, here, take them. I'll put on a pair of these jail slippers and go home.' He gave his boots to Detective Schoder voluntarily the night of the murder. They didn't take them. And Detective Schoder will have to admit that because he already has.

"Shell casings? What about the shell casings? It is a fact that seven shell casings were found in the creek bed and one shell casing was found in the loft. There are more .22 caliber shell casings, but they don't fit that gun. Why do you think the prosecutors didn't mention that to you?

"'Uh, I forgot,'" Sims said, imitating a bumbling sheriff's detective.

"The prosecutor told you that Bradford King called the operator the night of Diane's death and said he didn't know what was wrong with her. The prosecutor said Brad didn't ask for an ambulance, he asked for the police. There is going to be no proof of whether he asked for an ambulance or the police. What you are going to hear is that he called the operator. I don't know, I didn't grow up in the Sesame Street generation, I grew up with Howdy Doody and Captain Kangaroo. We were told to dial zero and get the operator and she will get you help. Bradford King dialed the operator and she did get him help. She did her best. But we all know Diane King was already dead. It was already over."

Sims was energized.

"The EMTs didn't know what had happened to Diane, either. When they first got there, they thought she had had a heart attack. It wasn't until they took part of her clothes off that they saw the bullet holes," he said, again stopping in front of the jury and shaking his head in amazement.

"Those are just a few things. I am not going to bore you to tears with a recitation of every circumstance that ever has occurred in Bradford King's life.

"But I am going to suggest to you that what is going to happen during this trial is an attempt by the prosecutor to assassinate Bradford King's character when it has never been put in issue. I'm not going to argue Bradford King's character.

"The only question here is who did it. That's the only issue: who did it? But the prosecutor is going to drag in everything he can to dirty up the case, make the jury confused, get them prejudiced. Because the prosecutor doesn't want you to do your job as you swore to do fairly and honestly, based upon the evidence you hear in this courtroom.

"They don't want you to do that. They want you to get mad at somebody (for Diane King's death) and take it out on Brad King. The prosecutor's case is full of suspicions, thoughts, opinions and beliefs—there are all of those things. But no facts. None."

CHAPTER 19

JOHN SIMS LEANED forward, his elbows resting on the defense table. His eyes darted around the courtroom, briefly focusing on Diane's family seated in the front row. He knew what they thought of him. He was their enemy. He was Brad's protector, his ally. He was the one person who was trying to prevent what they so desperately wanted: Brad King to spend the rest of his life in prison. Sims understood their anger. He had been a defense attorney long enough to accept that attitude from a victim's family.

He couldn't and wouldn't let it bother him. In fact, he was in a good mood as he waited for Sahli to call his first witness. He was pleased with his opening statement. But he also knew that it wasn't the key to winning the case. Sims had known for several weeks that Bradford King's defense would only be as strong as his cross-examination of the state's witnesses.

Although Sims hadn't admitted it, the general feeling among courthouse observers was that Brad would not take the witness stand. Brad's testimony would only open doors for the prosecution that had been slammed shut by Sindt's pre-trial rulings. Although Brad was eager to tell his side of the story, he had been in law enforcement long enough to know it wasn't the smartest thing to do.

188

Besides, he had given Detective Schoder two statements, each denying his involvement in Diane's death. Those tapes would be played for the jury. Many in the legal community who had already seen the statements believed Brad had won the battle with Schoder.

"They can't convict him on those statements alone, there has to be more," said one lawyer who was familiar with the case. "I don't think those statements hurt Brad that much at all."

There was also some speculation that Sims would not present any evidence. Instead, he would simply rely on his own ability to dismantle the state's case by discrediting key witnesses through cross-examination. Although Sims had only represented Brad for a few weeks, it was obvious he believed he had an opportunity to create enough doubt in the jury's mind to convince them to return a not guilty verdict.

The prosecution's opening statement did little to shake Sims' attitude. Sahli had rumbled through his opening statement like the leader of an armored division of well-trained military men. It was obvious he intended to grind it out, to bombard the jury with every minute detail of the two-year investigation.

Sims, on the other hand, was a lone rebel armed with a single automatic weapon. His sights were clearly set on the Calhoun County Sheriff Department's investigation of the case.

Detectives had acquired a lot of information, but it didn't mean anything if Sims could prove the sheriff department's initial investigation had been flawed. And based on what Sims had learned in reading the investigative reports, he didn't think he was going to have a problem proving it.

Where Sahli had been on the hot seat during opening statements, the pressure would clearly shift in the next few days to Detective Schoder and others in the sheriff's department.

Schoder, who had nervously roamed the halls during jury selection, was happy that the case was about to go to trial. For several months he had endured the vicious rumors about his ineptness. He never thought he had botched the investigation and wanted his day in court to prove his critics wrong.

"One way or the other, I want this over," he said, frustration creeping into his voice.

Inside the courtroom, spectators rustled noisily in their seats, restlessly anticipating the first witness.

Brad, as he had done during opening statements, remained stoic. He wore a dark blue suit. His legs weren't shackled and he wasn't handcuffed. However, a uniformed Calhoun County deputy was seated nearby.

Brad showed no emotion. Occasionally he would nod to someone in the audience, but he never acknowledged anyone in Diane's family, who sat a few feet away. When his eyes did meet those of Diane's relatives and friends, there was no response. Nothing.

His actions were just what prosecutors had hoped for. He appeared to be a smooth, calculating iceman. No anger, no fear, no remorse. Only a single-minded desire for acquittal.

Brad's demeanor would become a key issue at the trial. Sahli had used the word "demeanor" sparingly during his opening statement, but the word would resurface in almost every witness that Sahli would question.

What was Bradford King's demeanor? Sahli would ask. How did he act at the murder scene? At the funeral home? At the sheriff's department? At Western Michigan University?

What does it matter? Sims would always counter. Sims asked witnesses whether they had ever seen Brad grieve before. How do you know he wasn't grieving? Do you convict a man of murder simply because he doesn't show his grief the way you thought he should?

Those were just some of the questions the jury would have to deal with during the next few weeks.

Another question that concerned many involved in the trial was the jury's right to participate in the questioning of witnesses. Under Michigan law, jurors were allowed to take notes and ask questions of witnesses when the lawyers had finished their examination. The procedure worked this way: At the end of each witness's testimony, Sindt would ask the jury whether anyone had a question. If a juror did have a question, he would raise his hand. The juror would then privately write his question on a piece of paper and hand it to the bailiff. The judge and lawyers would then review the question at the bench to decide whether it was within the framework of the law. If it was, the judge would ask the question of the witness. If it wasn't, the question would be denied without explanation, and the lawyers would call the next witness.

It was a process that was highly unusual in a criminal case and it created another question mark in an already confusing and complicated case.

During the first few days of testimony, Sahli called a variety of law enforcement officers, emergency medical technicians and others who were at the murder scene or involved in Brad's initial call for help.

In addition to discussing the specific details of the murder scene, Sahli tried to demonstrate to the jury that Brad showed no emotion at the murder scene and did little, if anything, to revive his wife as she lay helplessly on the ground. He also focused on Brad's decision not to retrieve his children from the car, implying that Brad's actions were that of a cold, heartless man—a killer.

However, during cross-examination, Sims attempted to portray Brad as a professional law enforcement officer whose extensive training had taught him to stay away from the medical crews as they worked on Diane.

"He was doing what he was trained to do, wasn't he?" Sims asked. "He was staying out of the way of the emergency people while they worked on his wife."

Sims also pointed out that Brad didn't voluntarily remain on the porch, but did so because he had been ordered to stay there by one of the first deputies on the scene.

Joe Delapas, a Marshall dispatcher, was the first witness Sahli called. During direct examination, Delapas routinely explained what he had done when he received the emergency telephone call from Brad. His testimony was direct and uneventful. However, it changed when Sims questioned him.

"How did Mr. King act while you were on the telephone with him?" Sims asked.

"He was screaming and crying," Delapas said. "He was really upset. I could hardly understand him. He kept yelling and crying that he wanted to be with his wife and kept asking me why this had to happen."

Sahli, during re-direct, asked Delapas if Brad had ever indicated to him what had happened to Diane.

"No, he did not. He just kept crying and screaming that he wanted to be with her."

While Delapas' testimony seemed to help the defense, other emergency personnel and sheriff's deputies who were at the scene painted a different picture of Brad. To them, Brad was an uncaring, callous person.

"It didn't look like anything had been done to help her," said Jeffrey Caison. "It didn't appear she had been moved."

Caison also testified that when he had first arrived, he noticed two small children in the backseat of the car. One was an infant, the other 3 or 4 years old.

"The older child would occasionally put his face up to the window and look down at what we were doing," he said. "Then he would turn and look at the other, smaller child."

He said the children remained in the automobile the entire time they worked on Diane—about 15 minutes—and not once did Brad or anyone else attempt to remove the children from the vehicle.

"Did you know that Mr. King had been ordered by deputies to stay on the porch?" Sims asked.

"No. I did not know that," Caison answered.

Another emergency technician, Robert Mansfield, testified that he was shocked by Brad's actions that night.

"He seemed unconcerned, withdrawn," Mansfield said. "He didn't do the things that people normally do when someone they know or love is injured. They usually try to help. He didn't."

At one point, while Sahli was using slides to show the location of Diane's body at the murder scene, Brad turned away. He never looked at the slides. He placed his hand on his cheek, facing his chair toward the jury.

Sahli ended the first day of testimony by calling Deputy Guy Picketts, the first sheriff's deputy on the murder scene. Picketts, who had lived at the house as a young man, described the eerie scene of seeing Diane's body lying near the car and finding the two small children in the backseat.

"It appeared at first that the victim had fallen," he testified. "I didn't know then that she had been shot. I didn't find that out until a few minutes later. She had a little bit of blood around her nose, but that's all. I didn't observe anybody else at first, then I heard somebody yelling inside the house. It was Brad King. He was yelling at me to help his wife."

Picketts said that when he returned to Diane's side a short time later, he saw the children inside the car.

"They were in the backseat," he said. "The older one was looking out the window at his mother. He was crying."

*   *   *

A circumstantial case is only as strong as its weakest link, and one of the weakest links in Sahli's case was tying Brad to the murder weapon.

Although ballistics experts would say the shell casings found at the scene had been fired from the rifle found in the creek, they were unable to say positively that the bullets taken from Diane's body had come from that gun. They could say there was a strong possibility, but they couldn't swear to it. Their testimony was inconclusive.

It was the same with the ownership of the gun. Brad had readily admitted to owning a gun similar to the one found in the creek, but had told investigators he sold it in 1984, several years before the murder.

Sahli was prepared to call Barb Elgutta, Tom Darling, and Tom's son, Christopher Sly, to the witness stand. Each would testify that they had seen Brad with a gun similar to the rifle, but couldn't say positively that it was the same gun. In addition, each of those witnesses had some credibility problems. Barb was one of Diane's best friends. Rumors had described Darling as a main suspect in Diane's death. Sly was only 13 years old at the time and had only seen the gun once, when he was cutting the Kings' grass. Sahli was worried that Sims could discredit each of their testimonies.

What Sahli needed was an independent witness, someone unrelated to the case, to say they had seen that gun in Brad's possession.

Schoder and Stadfelt had left the courthouse and were on their way back to Marshall on the first day of testimony when they received an urgent radio message to return to the Battle Creek courthouse.

Upon arrival, they were met in the hallway by Detective Hough who informed them of an anonymous tip that had been received earlier that day on the Silent Observer line. The anonymous caller indicated that two women who had cleaned Brad's and Diane's house had recognized the murder weapon from media coverage of the case, but were afraid to come forward. The tipster gave authorities the names of the two women.

"We need you to check this out right away," Hough told the detectives. "It could be a big break."

After listening to the Silent Observer tape and acquiring photographs of the rifle, the detectives headed to a Battle Creek residence where one of the women lived. After a brief conversation, Lori Osten confirmed that she and her partner, Carol Mendez, had cleaned the Kings' townhouse in Battle Creek before Brad and Diane had moved to the farmhouse in early 1990.

Although Osten admitted to seeing "two long guns" in the basement of the Kings' residence, she couldn't say positively that one of the guns was the rifle.

"Truthfully, I don't know much about guns," she said.

However, Mendez did help the detectives when she arrived a few minutes later. She informed Schoder and Stadfelt that she was familiar with guns because she had purchased a 30.06 and a .20 gauge shotgun as gifts for her husband.

"I know a little bit about guns," she said.

Mendez said she had seen "a .22 rifle lying on the counter in the basement of their house. I know it was a .22 rifle because it had a real small barrel."

Schoder showed her a picture of the murder weapon along with the picture of a shotgun they took from Brad's house the night of Diane's murder.

"Is either one of them similar to what you saw in late 1989 or early 1990?" he asked.

She selected the rifle.

"It resembles what I saw on the counter because it's a .22 and the stock is dark wood," she said.

She told them that she hadn't come forward on her own because she was afraid of Brad.

"He makes me nervous," she said.

Mendez said another reason she had decided not to do anything was because she had been involved in her own brother's murder trial and didn't want to have to relive those memories again.

That was good enough for the detectives. They told the women their testimony was crucial and that they would have to accompany them to the prosecutor's office to discuss their testimony.

It was early evening when Sahli met with the women in his office in the Toeller Building across from the courthouse. He showed the women the actual rifle.

"Did it look like this?" he asked.

"It's similar," Mendez said. "It looks the same to me."

Sahli was ecstatic. Mendez was an independent witness who didn't even want to be involved in the case. It was obvious she was scared. Sahli knew her testimony would add strength and credibility to that of his other witnesses.

He told the women that it was likely they would have to testify. He said he intended to ask Sindt to allow him to include them as witnesses when the trial resumed the next day.

As expected, Sims wasn't happy when he found out about the new developments. No lawyer likes surprises in the middle of a trial, especially when the evidence could be so damaging to his client.

"It's late and it's improper," Sims said, asking Sindt to at least delay the ruling until he had an opportunity to interview the witnesses himself. Sims said the women might be describing pictures of a weapon they saw on television.

"We don't know what is going on here," he said. "I think it is wrong to allow them to testify."

Sindt declined to rule on Sahli's request until Tuesday.

"I'm not going to rule on this motion this morning," he said. "I want to give Mr. Sims the opportunity to interview the two witnesses."

Sahli was satisfied. Although he realized it was unusual to ask the court to allow him to add witnesses after the trial had begun, he felt confident the request was justified. It was obvious he hadn't known about the women until the previous day. He saw no reason why Sindt would not allow their testimony sometime during the trial.

"What are they going to come up with next?" a disgusted Sims said outside the courtroom. "This is ridiculous."

CHAPTER 20

DURING THE FIRST two days of testimony, Sahli had called 11 witnesses to the stand who did little more than provide the jury with a microscopic view of the murder scene. His witnesses, primarily Calhoun County sheriff's deputies, spent most of their time describing the routine police work that had occurred immediately after Diane's body was discovered. They did little to specifically tie Brad to the murder. If the case had ended now, Brad would walk out of the courtroom a free man.

During the morning session of the third day of the trial, Sahli called Michigan State Trooper Gary Lisle to the stand. It was Trooper Lisle and his dog, Travis, who had been summoned to the farmhouse an hour after Diane's body had been found. Lisle told the jury how he and Travis had tracked the murderer's circuitous route from the barn loft, through the fields behind the house and back onto Division Drive. Lisle admitted Travis had lost the trail near the driveway of the house, but he said that was because the trail had been tainted by the emergency crews and deputies who had arrived to help Diane King.

Lisle also described how he and his dog had returned two days later to follow the same track again from the loft to the fields and then to the creek bed, where the gun had been found.

198

Sims, who had been aggressive while questioning the first few witnesses, became combative during Lisle's testimony. He objected strenuously to Lisle's monologue regarding what he and Travis had done at the scene. Sims attacked Lisle's credibility and that of his German shepherd. He argued that the dog was not a bloodhound, but a tracking dog that had little experience in following human scents.

Disregarding Sims' strenuous objections, Sindt allowed Lisle's testimony. Although the minute details of the dog's ability to track and the discovery of the weapon were essential elements to building the state's case against Bradford King, Lisle's testimony was a bit tedious.

Following Lisle was Detective Jack Schoder, whose testimony would be anything but tedious.

For the first time since the trial began, the jury was going to have the opportunity to hear Brad's own statements to police. The statements would be presented to the jury through Schoder's testimony.

While Lisle had spent most of the morning inside the courtroom testifying, Schoder had worn a path in the halls outside the courtroom nervously pacing, waiting for his turn in the witness box. Schoder was restless. For almost two years he had lived with Diane King's murder. It had permeated not only his professional life, but his private life, too. In a way, his entire career as a police officer was on the line in this case. He knew more about the case than anybody else. He should be the state's star witness. But he knew he wouldn't be.

Because of the lengthy investigation and the fact that Sahli had refused to file charges for several months, everything Schoder had done during the investigation would be scrutinized. He felt he was on trial almost as much as Brad King was. If King were found not guilty, the blame would surely fall on him.

Schoder was even worried about his testimony during direct examination, which was unusual. Normally, detectives don't have to worry about questioning from their own district attorneys. But the animosity that had simmered between the investigating officers and the district attorney's office during the investigation had widened the gap between Sahli and Schoder.

They were no longer friends.

Schoder was obviously unhappy with Sahli's refusal to file charges for several months, and Sahli was equally upset with what he believed to be Schoder's sloppy investigation of the murder.

With competing thoughts swirling in his mind, Schoder finally walked to the witness stand at 1 P.M., Nov. 17, to begin the most arduous task of his professional life.

Schoder, a man in his mid-40s, shuffled nervously in his seat as Sindt gaveled the courtroom to order.

Before the tapes of Brad's statements were played, Sahli asked Schoder several questions surrounding his initial investigation. Schoder admitted that he hadn't considered Brad a suspect early in the case.

"I was consoling him for his loss," he said of the initial discussions he had with Brad. "I told him we were going to need his help in solving this crime because he was the only person on the property who could help us solve the murder."

Brad's first statement, as Schoder described it, was "informational" in nature.

"Like I said, he was not a suspect at that time," Schoder told Sahli.

However, Schoder said that two days later his opinion had changed. He began to consider Brad a key suspect, if not the only suspect.

For the first time during the trial, Brad displayed strong emotions, wiping tears from his eyes as the taped statements were played. Some of the jurors leaned forward in their seats, attempting to hear the tape, which was of extremely poor quality. Other jurors looked at

Brad as he wept at the sound of his own voice describing his discovery of Diane's body.

"Based on a lot of things, I am convinced that you are responsible for this," Schoder could be heard telling Brad on the tape. "You broke down, you cracked, you absolutely cracked and made a bad decision."

"I didn't kill my wife," Brad responded. "I didn't."

Spectators in the courtroom were mesmerized by the tape and surprised by Brad's expression of emotion. The spectators' eyes searched the courtroom for reactions from the other principals in the case. Sahli and Sims remained silent.

Sims did not appear to be upset with the tapes. Brad had made some mistakes, but Sims thought he could rectify those mistakes through cross-examination of other witnesses. Brad seemed pleased. He realized he had made some mistakes, but he was glad the jury had also heard him adamantly deny any role in his wife's death.

Schoder's biggest problem on the first day of his testimony came late in the day when he and Sims got into a heated exchange over Schoder's honesty on the witness stand.

While Sahli was questioning Schoder about a map Brad had drawn of the farmhouse and the surrounding area, Sims objected to the map and asked Sindt if he could "voir dire" Schoder about who had written several words on the map.

"Whose handwriting is on that map?" Sims asked.

"It's Brad King's handwriting," Schoder answered.

"Did you see Brad write those words on that map?" Sims asked, moving towards the witness stand.

"As I recall, yes."

"As you recall. Does that mean you are not certain?" Sims pushed forward.

"It's been a long time ago," Schoder answered.

"I know it's been a long time, that's the point," Sims said, turning his back on Schoder as he looked at the jurors, who were leaning forward in their seats.

"Brad drew the map and he would have put that writing on there," Schoder said.

"That's an assumption, sir," Sims said, his voice rising in anger. "I am asking you whether you recall actually seeing Bradford King write those words."

"Well, I know that Trooper Lisle . . ."

"Sir, can you answer my question directly," Sims interrupted, realizing he had Schoder confused and possibly trapped in a lie—a big mistake for the lead detective in a murder case.

"Did you see Brad King specifically write those words?" Sims asked, emphasizing every word.

Schoder hesitated. He stared at the small map for several excruciating seconds before responding, "Yes."

"Then you actually recall him writing those words," Sims said, again challenging Schoder's recollection.

"There again, sir, I can't recall who specifically wrote those words. I know that Trooper Lisle . . ."

"Wait just a minute, Officer," Sims said, confident that he now had Schoder on the run. "You just got through telling this jury that you did specifically recall him writing those words. Now what is it?"

"As I recall, Brad drew the map."

"Answer my question," Sims said in a scolding tone. "Who wrote the words? I have asked the question about five times, can you please answer it?"

"I guess I don't recall specifically if Brad or Trooper Lisle wrote the words on there."

"So when you told this jury moments ago that Brad King had specifically written those words on there, you were lying? Weren't you?"

"No, I was not . . ." Schoder said, attempting to explain until Sims interrupted again.

"You were mistaken then, is that it?" Sims said, smiling at the jury. "Sir, I have heard your excuses several times. Can you simply answer the question?"

Schoder looked at Sims, then toward Sahli. Both simply looked back at him. He never looked at the jury.

"I don't recall," Schoder finally said quietly.

"Then you did lie to me," Sims said, moving his head up and down as he looked toward the jury. "No further questions."

Despite Sims' angry exchange with Schoder, Sindt allowed Sahli to introduce the map. Sims didn't care. The map was not important. What was important was the fact that he had forced Schoder to admit in front of the jury that he gave a specific answer when, in fact, he really did not know that answer to be true.

The exchange was an accident. Sims was simply asking a routine question on the admittance of a piece of evidence when he realized that Schoder had made a mistake. It was a fortuitous break, and something he hoped the jury would not forget when he began his cross-examination of Schoder later in the trial.

Sahli simply shook his head in disgust.

The hours seemed to drag on unmercifully for Schoder. Because of court delays, the trial did not resume until 1 P.M. the following day. Schoder had always known that Sims was going to be rough on him, but he was really worried now because Sims had had almost 24 hours to formulate a plan of attack on cross-examination.

Sims, too, was edgy. He was intent on discrediting Schoder. He had been disgusted at Schoder's testimony during questioning by Sahli, and he wasn't going to allow Schoder to walk away without taking responsibility for the numerous mistakes he believed had been made in the investigation.

The mood for Sims' cross-examination had been set the day before when he accused Schoder of lying under oath to help the state's case.

With that confrontation fresh in his mind, Schoder went back to the witness stand to undergo questioning by Sims. Where Sahli had spent most of his time asking Schoder about things he did do during the investigation, Sims was intent on focusing the jury's attention on what Schoder didn't do.

Schoder's credibility as an investigator was a key to the defense's case. And if Sims had his way, Schoder would be stripped of credibility as an investigator by the time he left the witness stand.

Standing at the podium, directly in front of Schoder, Sims shuffled through a stack of handwritten notes he had made during Schoder's direct examination. Sims took a deep breath, then began.

"Sir, you were the head of the investigation into this matter on Feb. 9, 1991, correct?" Sims asked almost immediately.

"In part," Schoder answered nervously.

"You and Detective Stadfelt. Correct? You were the lead detectives. And weren't you relieved of that duty?" Sims asked, his eyes focusing on Schoder.

"I'm not sure what you mean?"

"You were relieved as the head of this investigation," Sims said harshly. He refused to waste time playing word games with Schoder. "Was it April of 1991 or June of 1991? It was one of those two dates, wasn't it?"

"Yes it was."

"And it was taken over by this gentlemen sitting here at this counsel table, wasn't it?" Sims said, pointing to Gary Hough, the detective with the Michigan State Police who had been called in to organize the investigation several months after the killing. "He replaced you, didn't he?"

"Yes."

"So you got fired, taken off the job, didn't you?" Sims pursued.

"No, sir," Schoder answered, a smile crossing his face. "I wasn't fired."

"You were relieved, and you became a member of the task force, right?" Sims said, irritated by Schoder's smile.

Whether Schoder's smile was a nervous reaction or not, Sims didn't care. He was serious. Schoder was the most important witness in the trial for the defense.

"That's correct," Schoder said, the smile disappearing from his face.

Sims paused, perusing the stack of notes he had prepared for his cross-examination. He then pursued a string of questions designed to further cloud Schoder's investigation. He questioned him about his whereabouts the evening of the murder.

"Weren't you at some kind of party?" Sims asked.

"Yes. A Valentine's Day party," Schoder said.

"Did you have a lot to drink there?" he asked.

"About a third of a drink, whiskey," he said.

"Hmm," Sims responded before moving on. There had been no indication throughout the case that Schoder had been drunk the night of the murder, Sims was simply attempting to rattle Schoder. A defensive witness could be extremely damaging for a prosecutor's case.

Again Sims paused. He looked briefly at the jury before beginning his next line of questioning which concerned the handling of the threatening letter Diane had received.

Sims thought Schoder's investigation of the threatening letter opened a door for the defense. If he wanted the jury to believe that Brad was innocent, he was going to have to give the jury something else to focus on. His best avenue was still the stalker theory. In addition to what he thought was a flawed murder investigation, he also thought Schoder had done an equally bad job in investigating the threatening letter Diane had received.

"You were the detective handling the investigation involving a letter received by Mrs. King, correct?"

"Yes."

"When you got the letter, of course, you sent it off to the FBI, right?" Sims asked, feigning ignorance.

"No, I did not."

"You didn't?" Sims asked, acting surprised. "Well, did you wiretap the phone of the Kings or put a tracer on it?"

"No sir, I did not."

"Did you put a tracer or wiretap on the phone at WUHQ-TV, Channel 41?"

"No, we did not."

"Did you interview every employee at WUHQ, Channel 41?"

"No."

"Did you interview the friends and family of Diane King?"

"No, we did not."

"Did you interview the friends and family of Bradford King?"

"No, we did not."

"Did you check out other people who had written to celebrities of that type and talk to them about whether they had had any contact with Diane King?"

"I did talk to one person during that investigation."

"When was that? Before or after Diane King was dead?"

"I don't recall."

"It was after, wasn't it?" Sims said, angrily.

"I don't recall."

"Did you investigate the personal lives of Brad King and his wife at that time?"

"No, I did not, sir."

"Did you send the letter off to the Michigan State Crime Lab?"

"No, I did not, sir."

"Did you do spot checks on Diane King or surveillance around the clock at that time?"

"No, I did not."

Sims paused. He turned to the jury with a quizzical look on his face. A look of disbelief.

"Do you know if anyone at the Calhoun County Sheriff's Department did any of those things?"

"Any of those things?" Schoder responded sarcastically, putting the emphasis on the last two words. "No sir."

Sims questioned Schoder's efforts to locate the identity of fingerprints found on the letter. Schoder defended his actions, disagreeing with Sims on the time frame of the investigation. He admitted he had difficulty tracking down Cindy Accusta's husband, Juan, who had handled the letter the night Diane found it.

"Okay, you were trying," Sims said, shaking his head. "But you did all this after Diane King was dead, right?"

"No."

Sims again paused. He didn't pursue that any further. He believed he had made his point with the jury. To him, it was obvious that the sheriff's department hadn't taken the threatening letter that seriously. Sims moved on to Brad's statements to Schoder.

The tapes had been played by Sahli during Schoder's direct examination. Sahli had pinpointed several aspects of the statement which had helped him. Now Sims had his turn. "Do you remember saying this, Detective Schoder?" Sims said, reading from a transcript of Brad's second statement:

"I'll tell you Brad, you know this as well as I do. We're both adult men here. You know there is a fine line between love and hate. Sometimes you can cross over that line. You add up the pressures of life. You've got your part-time job, you've recently lost your job with the probation department. Some other things aren't going quite well for you. Brad, I can understand why things can fall apart and your wheels can come tumbling off and I think that you probably need some counseling yourself."

Sims stopped reading and looked toward Schoder.

"Do you remember that part of your question?" Sims asked.

"Yes sir."

"Were you trying to indicate to him or insinuate that he was possibly insane?"

"No sir."

"What were you doing?"

Schoder looked at him for a moment.

"Trying to find out the truth."

Sims didn't miss a beat. "Really?" he said, moving to another area of obvious importance: Brad's repeated assertions that he hadn't killed Diane.

"Let's turn to the denials," Sims said, raising his voice for emphasis. "That's important. If I count them, I see approximately 27 denials in his second statement. Would you disagree that there are approximately 27 denials by Mr. King in this statement alone?"

"I wouldn't disagree with that, Counsel," Schoder said.

"Twenty-seven denials," Sims said with great emphasis. "Twenty-seven denials. And by your testimony in this courtroom, you consider that a soft denial, is that correct?"

"Yes."

"If he had only denied it 10 times, is that a confession, in your mind? " Sims said, as he looked at the jury.

"No sir. I would not think that is a confession."

"Excuse me for a moment, I'm trying to get your scale here, sir," Sims said, sarcastically. "If 27 is a soft denial, then is five a confession? If you say five times, 'I didn't do it,' that's a confession."

"No sir."

"Does it get to be a moderate denial when it gets to 50?"

"No sir."

"Why do you consider 27 times a soft denial?" Sims asked increduously.

"Because he didn't get irate with me," Schoder said. "He was not mad or upset at all with me when I accused him of the murder."

Sims looked at him and shook his head.

"I suppose you would have preferred that he got up and pounded you in the teeth and then you could have arrested him and held him in jail and sweated him some more, right? That would have been a strong denial, wouldn't it."

Before Schoder could answer, Sahli was on his feet, objecting. It was the first time Sahli had objected to anything that Sims had asked Schoder all afternoon.

Sindt upheld Sahli's objection.

"That's argumentative, Mr. Sims," Sindt said.

"Would it have been a strong denial if he had got up and punched you in the teeth?" Sims continued, practically ignoring Sindt's ruling seconds earlier.

Again Sahli objected.

"Judge, I just objected to that very question and you sustained my objection," Sahli said, raising his hands upwards to indicate helplessness.

Sindt, who had been calm and focused during the trial, looked at Sims with a hint of anger and frustration.

"Mr. Sims, where are you going with this? What's the relevance?" Sindt asked.

"Judge, I'm trying to get this witness to explain whether there was a denial or not," Sims answered.

"I think this had been asked and answered numerous times," Sindt said. "It's cumulative at this point. I am going to sustain Mr. Sahli's objection."

"I understand, your honor, but I am attempting to cross-examine in my own style and that's what I'd like to do," Sims said, peeved at Sindt's intrusion into his cross-examination.

"Well, I've ruled."

"And I accept the Court's ruling."

Sims moved on.

"You did not take Mr. King's boots from him as they have said here in court, did you? He volunteered them to you that night."

"Yes."

"In fact, you gave him a pair of those little jail house slippers to walk home in, right?"

"Yes," Schoder said.

"Did you call in the Michigan State Police crime lab that evening?"

"No, we did not."

"Did you impose security around the premises? Did you cordon it off?"

"No sir, we did not. Based on our information we had at the time, we had completed our research."

"You said you were there and conducted a search and there was nobody there so you left. When you left, did you even bother to lock the door?"

"I don't recall. I don't believe I was the one who secured the house."

"So, to your knowledge, nobody even shut the door?"

"The doors were shut."

"To your knowledge, or are you offering something you really don't know again?" Sims asked, referring to the earlier skirmish over truthfulness. "How do you know?"

"I was there when we left."

"I thought you said just a minute ago that you weren't?" Sims asked, his voice becoming argumentative.

"There were several of us there at the time, sir. When we left the property, I wasn't the one who pulled the door shut. The doors were shut when we left."

"But you didn't shut the doors."

"That's correct."

"You certainly, you didn't lock them. Right?"

"Correct."

"Didn't put a guard on the premises?"

"That's correct."

"Didn't cordon off the driveway and put a police car out front to keep people from going out there?"

"That's correct."

"You don't have any idea whether people came in there the minute you walked out of there, or five minutes after you left or not, do you?"

"That's correct."

"And you don't know who it might have been?"

"That's correct, sir."

Sims questioned Schoder about running any tests on Brad's hands that night to determine whether he had fired a weapon. Schoder indicated he hadn't.

Once again, the fact that Schoder hadn't done something was more important than what he had done.

"And you didn't even take pictures or make casts of the footprints that you were aware of out back?"

"That's correct."

"Why? Isn't it because you had already determined within five minutes of getting there that night, that Mr. King was the suspect?"

"No sir."

"Well, you told Bradford King in the second statement, 'I've been working on this for a day-and-a-half and I don't have an answer.' A whole day-and-a-half and you didn't have an answer. Golly, a whole day-and-a-half."

Schoder smiled at Sims' emphasis. Before he could answer, Sims was asking another question.

"You had already singled him out and you were trying to get him to confess, weren't you?" Sims demanded.

"On the 11th? Yes sir."

"So, even before the gun was found, you had made up your mind that he was the key suspect," Sims said, continuing to focus on the point that less than 48 hours after the murder, Schoder had dismissed anyone else as a possible suspect.

"Let's say I was very suspicious at that time, yes."

"Isn't it true that from that point on you never really ever pursued any other suspect?"

"No sir," Schoder said, adding that he had checked other leads.

"But, really, there were no other suspects in your mind from that point on, were there?" Sims asked.

"That's correct."

"But you didn't arrest him until almost one year after he was determined to be the main suspect?" Sims again asked.

"That's correct, sir."

"Why?"

"You'll have to ask somebody else that question," Schoder said.

Sims also accused Schoder of lying to Brad during the tape recorded statements.

"You lied to him, didn't you?" Sims said. "You told him half-truths. You deceived him, you told him they could tie the gun to him and you knew they couldn't, didn't you? You told him lies?"

"I didn't think what I told him were falsehoods," Schoder responded.

"Right, just like you didn't believe yesterday that the writing on that piece of paper was put there by Mr. King?"

"I couldn't recall if Mr. King did it or Trooper Lisle did it," Schoder said, still defensive.

"But you continued to say it until you got caught in the fib, right?"

"I was just trying to explain to the jury," Schoder said.

"And you would try to explain this situation (that you lied to Brad about tying him to the gun) to the jury because you've got no proof and never have had any proof that Bradford King committed this murder?"

"I don't understand what you are saying," Schoder said.

"Never mind," Sims said disgustedly.

Schoder had been prepared to defend his actions, but what he wasn't prepared for was a question Sims asked near the end of his questioning. Sims caught Schoder completely off guard, once again questioning his investigative abilities.

"Detective Schoder, did you even know that Mrs. King had made a complaint in November 1990 to the Battle Creek Police that she was being followed by two men in a car?" Sims asked. "Did you know that?"

"I'm not familiar with that," Schoder said, obviously caught off-guard.

"You never heard of that?" Sims asked. "The lead detective, and you didn't hear about that? Did you ever ask Mr. King about that?"

"I haven't had any contact with Mr. King since Feb. 11, 1991," Schoder said.

Sims again paused, looked directly at Schoder and asked: "Is your conscience bothering you, Detective Schoder?"

"No sir," Schoder said firmly.

"Isn't it a fact, Detective Schoder, that you just didn't do your job?" Sims said, shaking his head as he gathered his notes together. "I have no further questions of this witness."

Sindt turned to the jury as he had done after every witness had finished testifying.

"Anyone have any questions?"

One juror raised his hand. The bailiff took the folded question and handed it to Sindt. He immediately called the two attorneys to the bench.

Outside earshot of the jury, Sindt showed them the question. The juror had heard Schoder ask Brad on the taped statement if he would take a polygraph test. Although Brad did not give an answer then, the juror wanted to know now.

Sims was furious. He wanted a mistrial. The question should never have been left on the tape. It was improper.

The attorneys couldn't ask about it, and neither should the jury.

Sindt was in a jam. It was a question that could force a mistrial. He decided to take the afternoon recess. He needed to think about the possible problem and what to do about it.

Because the discussion was held at the bench, no one else in the courtroom knew of the new, and possibly explosive development. The attorneys for both sides wore grim faces as they returned to their seats.

"Let's take the afternoon recess," a frustrated Sindt announced to the courtroom.

Outside the courtroom, a tired and disheveled Schoder leaned against the wall. He avoided contact with Diane's family or members of the district attorney's office. His testimony had been the low point of the trial, and he didn't want to face them.

It was obvious that he was upset that Sahli hadn't attempted to protect him from Sims' onslaught. Several times, Sahli could have stopped Sims' attacks with a simple objection.

However, he had patiently remained in his seat calmly watching Sims as he tore into Schoder. Whether because of trial strategy or his anger over continuing problems between the prosecutor's office and the sheriff's department, Sahli hadn't moved a muscle to protect Schoder. And Schoder needed the protection.

"What did you expect?" a friend who was consoling Schoder asked. "If he loses the case, who do you think is going to get blamed for it? He can say he did his best, but you guys blew it for him."

Schoder shrugged his shoulders.

"I guess when you look at it, he really wasn't that bad on me," Schoder said with great understatement. "I expected a lot worse."

CHAPTER 21

SAHLI HAD CALLED approximately 35 witnesses by the time the trial entered its fourth week. His circumstantial case was strong. The testimony had been tedious at times, but the case against Brad King was getting clearer with each piece of evidence. Although Sims had won several legal skirmishes, Sahli was still able to provide the jury with numerous pieces of evidence that pointed to Brad King's guilt.

Common sense was all Sahli would ask the jury to use in piecing together the evidence. Through the testimony of a variety of witnesses, mostly law enforcement officers, the jury now knew several key elements about the case:

They knew that Brad was the only person who had known when Diane was coming home from Detroit the evening she was killed.

They knew that Brad hadn't expected the children to be with her.

They knew that Diane, because of the threatening letter and telephone calls, had taken extra security precautions when she approached the farmhouse. Included in the precautions was her refusal to get out of her car at the house unless she saw Brad. If she knew Brad was not going to be at home, she would ask friends to accompany her home and then she would circle the yard around the farmhouse to make sure the doors and windows hadn't been tampered with.

The jury was aware that the rifle found in the creek behind the house was probably the murder weapon, although ballistics experts couldn't say positively that it was. They did know the shell casing found in the barn loft had been fired from that weapon.

They knew through Trooper Lisle's testimony that the likelihood that someone besides Brad King had been on the property the night of Diane's murder was minimal. Lisle said the track Travis had followed contradicted statements Brad had given to Schoder concerning his walk on the property that evening.

They knew that Calhoun County sheriff's deputies had made several mistakes in the initial investigation, including failing to take pictures or plaster casts of footprints in the snow behind the house and failing to secure the scene when they left that night.

They knew that on the day Diane was killed Brad had rented a video, "Next of Kin," a movie about a Chicago police officer who is at odds with relatives over the murder of a family member.

They had heard several neighbors of the Kings testify that they hadn't heard any gunshots on the day Diane was killed. Their testimony directly contradicted statements Brad had given to Schoder indicating he had "heard gunshots off and on all day." They also knew that the neighbors had not seen any strangers in the area that day.

They knew that Tom Darling and Chris Sly had seen a gun similar to the murder weapon in Brad's possession a few months prior to Diane's death. And they also knew, from the testimony of Brad's mother, Marjorie Lundeen, and his brother, Scott, that Brad's grandfather had given Brad a .22 caliber rifle similar to the murder weapon when he was a young man.

What the jury didn't know about statements concerning the gun also helped Sahli.

Despite Sims' vigorous protestations, Sindt would not allow him to cross-examine Darling on rumors that had circulated through the community about he and Diane.

Sims thought Darling's testimony would be viewed with much less credibility if he were allowed to show the jury that Darling had a motive to tie Brad to the gun. If Brad was convicted, the rumors would stop, Sims theorized. If Brad wasn't convicted, Darling would again be involved in community speculation about his involvement in the murder.

"I think it goes to the weight of his testimony," Sims argued.

Sindt denied Sims' motion, saying it wasn't relevant to the case at hand.

Sahli was ecstatic. That ruling, coupled with Sindt's earlier decision to let the two cleaning women testify about the gun they had seen in the Kings' apartment, solidified Sahli's belief that he had sufficiently tied the rifle to Brad.

Although Sahli had won battles on several fronts, many problems were still just over the horizon.

By all estimates, the state's case against Bradford King was moving with a dangerous lack of speed. Not only was Sahli having a difficult time getting some of his key evidence before the jury, he also found himself fighting motions from the defense that threatened to end the trial.

Sims' repeated motions for mistrial, coupled with his relentless attempts to derail even the most innocuous testimony, had greatly lengthened the trial. Court officials were now estimating that it might take two months to complete the case.

Judge Sindt was concerned. With the massive media coverage surrounding the case and the fact that Court TV was broadcasting the trial live into a majority of the homes in Calhoun County, the chance of a juror becoming "tainted" by outside influences was getting stronger every day.

Sindt also had other things to worry about. He knew Sahli was moving into a critical area of the trial where the couple's friends, relatives and coworkers would be called to the witness stand. They would attempt to testify about a myriad of issues, including marital discord, Brad's demeanor before and after the funeral and, if Sahli had his way, Brad's affairs with several coeds.

While Sahli had been painstakingly building his circumstantial case, Sims had been laying the groundwork for an appeal. Although his focus was winning an acquittal for Brad now, he was also preparing the record for the appellate courts.

"There's error all over the place," he said outside the courtroom.

Sims had asked for six different mistrials in the first three weeks of testimony. The juror's question about Brad taking the polygraph test was the most important. After lengthy discussions, both inside the courtroom and in the judge's chambers, Sindt overruled Sims' request. Sindt said he would handle the problem with a specific instruction to the jury prior to their deliberations.

Sims had also asked for mistrials on issues ranging from inadmissable statements made by a witness in front of the jury to buttons worn in the courtroom by members of Diane's family. The buttons displayed a picture of Diane and had been recommended by a victim's support group in Battle Creek.

Sims was livid when he saw the buttons. He called them inflammatory. "It's like allowing the state to have a banner in the courtroom," he said.

After much discussion, Sindt again denied Sims' motion for a mistrial, but did order the family not to wear the buttons inside the courtroom again. Diane's family and friends still were allowed to wear the buttons in the hallway, outside the view of the jury.

"We just wanted to show the jury that Diane's still alive in our hearts," her sister, Darlene, explained. "It's important for them to know who she was and that she was important to us."

Sims had also asked for a mistrial when one of Diane's close friends inadvertently made a statement in front of the jury that Sindt had previously ruled was inadmissable. During questioning by Sahli, Joanne Karaba told the jury without being asked that Diane had suspected Brad of being the person who had called her at work, implying that Diane didn't become concerned about a possible stalker until she received the threatening letter.

"Diane told me she thought Brad was playing a sick joke," Karaba said of the telephone calls to the television station. "We laughed about that."

Sims, who had been battling Sahli throughout the trial to prevent witnesses from offering inadmissable evidence, was angered by her comments. Rather than immediately object and draw additional jury attention to the statements, Sims waited a few minutes before raising the objection. When he did, it was apparent the battles with Sahli were taking their toll. Sims appeared weary of the constant battles.

He accused Sahli of attempting to circumvent the court's earlier rulings about admissable evidence. He accused Sahli of prosecutorial misconduct.

"He forged ahead when he knew what she was going to say," Sims angrily told Sindt outside the jury's presence. "It is a clear statement that he elicited. It is in violation of this court's ruling and I want a mistrial. It's his misconduct."

Sahli, obviously concerned about Karaba's statement, responded that she had offered the information on her own.

"Her answer wasn't based on anything I asked," Sahli said defensively. "I didn't elicit that response."

After a lengthy discussion, Sindt again denied the mistrial.

In a bizarre twist, Sims also accused Diane's brother, Allen, of stalking Brad as he was being transported to and from the courtroom. Sims told the court that Allen was armed with a buck knife and had taken threatening stances in the hallway and outside the building while Brad was being moved from the courtroom to the county jail.

Although Allen laughed off Sims' accusations, it was clear the trial was raising anxiety levels in everyone.

Sindt ordered deputies to search everyone entering the courtroom and told them to take extra security precautions. He also ordered that no weapons, including legal ones, be allowed in the courthouse.

"It's a joke. I never threatened him," Allen said outside the court as he removed the buck knife strapped to his side. "I wasn't going to harm him. I just wanted him to see the face of Diane's family every time he came in. I wanted him to know I am here to see that justice is done."

While Allen was being macho, other family members were becoming increasingly frightened with each motion for a mistrial. In the halls outside the courtroom, several family members wondered openly how long it would be before Sindt was forced to declare a mistrial and order Brad retried before a new jury.

If he was forced to grant a mistrial, everyone associated with the case knew the new trial wouldn't be held in Calhoun County. Because of the massive publicity covering the first four weeks of this trial, it would be impossible to select an impartial jury for a second trial.

Sahli was acutely aware of that and, after Karaba's mistake and Allen's alleged confrontation with Brad, he instructed each witness and Diane's family and friends to be extremely careful in what they said and did in and around the courtroom.

"The last thing we want or can afford is a mistrial," he told his assistants to tell the witnesses. "Make sure they listen to what I say and tell them to respond accordingly."

Sahli had two days before Thanksgiving break, and he wanted to give the jury something to consider over the holidays. He had presented his circumstantial evidence. Now he was prepared to move into the emotional, human side of his case: testimony from Diane's family and friends.

Through their testimony, Sahli hoped to show how Diane's life had deteriorated from one of hope and happiness to fear and frustration in a matter of months, starting with the threatening letter on Halloween Eve and ending with her death on Feb. 9. It was important for Sahli to show that the couple's marriage was in turmoil—Diane was angry over Brad's inability to keep a job, and that was causing marital difficulties.

This wouldn't be easy. Using the Karaba incident as his justification, Sims urged Sindt to use extreme caution in allowing Sahli to question the witnesses.

"The prosecution has backdoored me at every opportunity," Sims said, indicating he didn't want another "mistake" by a witness to get testimony in front of the jury. "I don't want to keep fighting the back door as well as the front door. There are three or four witnesses coming up that I am really concerned about."

Freida Newton, Diane's mother, was one of them. The others were women Brad had affairs with. They were all scheduled to testify within the next few days.

Sims' protestations and Sindt's concern about a mistrial caused the trial to sputter and stop on several occasions. A pattern developed. Nearly every witness would be called to the stand and asked a few brief questions. Sims would object and the jury would be ordered from the courtroom. Sindt would then force Sahli to question the witness as if the jury were in the courtroom. Objections would be made, they would argue those objections and Sindt would rule on what the witness could and couldn't say. After that was settled, the jury would be returned to the courtroom and the examination would resume.

It was burdensome, to say the least.

The key witnesses Sahli called on Tuesday were one of Diane's best friends, Kristina Mony, and Diane's sister, Denise Verrier. Each testified about the goals Diane had in life. They talked of Diane's desire, over Brad's adamant objections, to quit her job in June and stay at home with her children. They talked about Diane's desire to develop a program designed to promote Native American tradition in elementary and secondary schools.

Denise admitted during her testimony that Diane had confided in her that she and Brad weren't getting along and that they needed time alone to work out their problems.

They also described Brad's demeanor at the funeral home. They said he was artificial, cold-hearted and distant.

"I didn't feel comfortable around him," said Mony, who stated she had been best friends with both Brad and Diane. "He was cold. It wasn't the Brad I used to know. He had changed. He had always appeared before to be a warm and caring person. But it was clear to me he wasn't that way any longer. He seemed distant, like he didn't want to have anything to do with any of Diane's friends."

For the first time in the trial, emotion overwhelmed the courtroom. So far the witnesses, mostly law enforcement officers, had been detached from the emotions resulting from Diane's murder. However, with Kristina Mony, the mood changed.

She broke down and cried when Sahli asked his first question, and she continued to sob throughout her entire testimony.

"I'm sorry," the young college student apologized. "It's hard for me. I loved Diane."

During cross-examination, her tears became Brad's tears as they both sat openly wiping their eyes.

"Ma'am, would it be fair for me to say that at the time you appeared at the funeral, you had no information about what had gone on with Brad King's life since the death of his wife only a couple of days before?" Sims asked.

"None," she said.

"You didn't know that he had been questioned twice and accused of murder?" he asked. "You didn't know that his house had been searched and that his personal life had been turned upside down? You didn't know that he was in arguments with his mother-in-law about where his kids were going to go and who was going to take them? But you did know that he had lost his wife. And you knew that family, and you liked them very much?"

"Very much," she said, beginning to sob heavily. "I loved both of them very much . . . Brad called to wish me good luck on my prom night. I babysat for their children. They were my friends."

She looked at Brad, who also began to cry. Sims paused while Mony fought to hold back her tears.

"I understand," he said, walking back to the defense table.

The mood in the courtroom changed drastically during Sims' confrontational cross-examination of Denise Verrier.

Through Denise and later through Freida, Sims hoped to show the jury how much dislike the family had for Brad, even before Diane's murder. It was his theory that part of the reason Brad had even been charged with the crime was the family's desire to retain custody of Diane's children.

If Brad wasn't convicted, he would get permanent custody of the children—one court had already ordered Freida to return the children to Brad shortly after Diane's death. To Sims, it was just another example of the massive power of the state focused against Brad King.

"Mrs. Verrier, you don't really like Brad King at all, do you?" Sims said, walking toward the witness stand.

"At this point or before?" she answered firmly.

"At this point," Sims said.

"He is accused of murdering my sister," she said. "I don't care for that at all."

Sims accused her of spreading word around the funeral home that he had better not try to take the children away from them.

"You and your mother had already decided that the kids were going to live with your mother, and your family had decided they were going to do anything they could to make sure Brad didn't keep his own children, right?" Sims asked, his voice rising in anger.

"No," she said firmly, but sarcastically. "Not at all."

"Didn't there almost immediately following the burial of Diane ensue a major fight between Brad King and your family over the custody of those children?" Sims asked. "Didn't your mother in fact insist on taking the children home after the funeral? And she didn't send them back, did she? Not until a court ordered it. Isn't that right?"

"Yes."

Throughout the trial witnesses had talked about Diane's stubbornness, her ability to stand up to adversaries. Now the jury was getting a glimpse of that strong personality from Denise. She was unyielding in the face of Sims' attacks. She had her side of the story to tell and she was going to tell it. As she argued with Sims, family members leaned forward in their seats to offer her encouragement.

"You always want to call him the defendant, but isn't he your brother-in-law?" Sims said as he continued to attempt to fluster Denise.

"He was, not any more," she said angrily.

"Let's get it straight, you hate him, don't you?" Sims asked.

"No, I hate what has happened to my sister," she said.

Denise's testimony Tuesday set the stage for Freida's testimony on Wednesday, and the courtroom was packed for the first time since the trial began. Even Court TV didn't keep the spectators away. Everyone wanted to see Freida, the strong-willed matriarch of the Newton clan.

Sahli had a plan for Wednesday, the day before the Thanksgiving break. He wanted to send the jury home to their families with a clear picture of Diane King's home life.

Purposefully, he had scheduled Freida Newton and Julie Cook as his last two witnesses before the break. Freida, the devastated mother, and Julie, the coed who, by her own admission, had slept with Brad before and after Diane's death, would provide the jury with a view of Brad's double life.

Even if Sindt wouldn't allow him to get into the specific details of Brad's sexual trysts, at least Sahli could make it clear to the jury that Brad had more on his mind than being a loving husband and father of Diane and the children.

Where Denise had been polite, but forceful, Freida seemed angry and mean. Freida was not a good witness. She was contemptuous of Brad and his attorney. She was argumentative, even with Sahli. Her hatred was apparent. Anything she said was cloaked in the belief that she would do anything to see Brad in prison and away from his children. It was difficult to feel sorry for her, and that frustrated Sahli because he wanted the jury to sympathize with her.

Any hopes that Sahli had held earlier in the day for a dramatic finish to the week's testimony were gone. It was a frustrating afternoon.

Julie Cook's expected testimony did not materialize. Although she took the witness stand, she didn't testify before the jury. Sahli was blocked by Sims at every turn. Sims argued that Cook's testimony was irrelevant and was offered by Sims only to "portray Brad as a bad character."

"Her testimony has nothing to do with who committed this murder," he argued. "It is simply presented to show that Brad was a bad person because he was having an affair. How many bad acts do they have to attribute to Brad before the jury makes the stretch that because he has done all these other bad things, he must have committed the murder?"

Sindt agreed, saying he would not allow her to discuss anything even remotely related to the affairs. Instead of continuing the argument, Sahli simply removed Cook from the stand. He indicated that he would call her to the witness stand when the trial resumed next week. That would give him additional time to research the legal issues and prepare for one of the final battles of the trial.

Instead of entering the holidays with confidence and satisfaction, Wednesday's setbacks had left Sahli facing a five-day weekend buried in troubling questions.

Sims was tired, too. It had been a long four weeks. He had fought hard to keep a large amount of testimony from the jury, but it was obvious the evidence was mounting.

CHAPTER 22

THE TRIAL RESUMED on Tuesday, Dec. 1. The five-day break had given everyone, including the jury, a chance to catch their breath for the final leg of what had become a marathon trial.

There were also expectations that the state's case was about to end. A quick glance at the witness list revealed few significant witnesses left to testify. Unless there was a major problem, the state's case would likely be completed by the end of the week. If Sims intended to put on any evidence, and no one knew for sure if he would, the trial might go an additional week at the most. Then there would be closing arguments and, everyone hoped, a verdict.

Everyone attending the trial could see the end, including Brad, who appeared unusually chipper. Mrs. Lundeen, Brad's mother, had been a study of grace under pressure. She had supported him with quiet strength and dignity as witness after witness testified against him. He looked at her on this day and winked. She smiled back at him.

Sahli and Sims started the day as they had on many days during the trial: arguing about the testimony regarding Brad's extramarital affairs. Most prosecutors would have given up on the issue, but Sahli kept trying. The setback with Julie Cook the week before did little to discourage him. He came back to court Tuesday armed with additional case law and renewed energy. He intended to call Cook and Anne Hill today, and he again asked Sindt to allow him to fully explore all aspects of their relationship with Brad, citing numerous cases from throughout the United States.

"We are offering this to prove marital discord," Sahli argued. "We are not offering it to show a bad act. We think this is relevant testimony to assist the jury in determining a motive. Brad wasn't happy in his marriage and he told these women that on numerous occasions. It's important and it's relevant."

Sims disagreed.

"We can't isolate ourselves from reality," he told Sindt. "This testimony is coming in the back door to prove that Brad is a bad person and that's all. As I said many times before, it's inadmissable and improper testimony."

Once again, Sindt agreed. He told Sahli he would allow Cook and Hill to testify, but not specifically about the affairs. He said the women could testify about what Brad had told them about his life, including the lies about being a single parent and father.

"The statements about his marriage are admissable," Sindt said. "That goes to marital discord. There will be no testimony about the affairs."

Before Sahli could bring the two women to the stand, he had some other unfinished business to take care of. In rapid succession, Sahli called several of Diane's co-workers from Grand Junction and Battle Creek to the stand—but they presented conflicting views of the couple. While friends from Grand Junction seemed to describe Brad and Diane as a happy couple, the witnesses from Battle Creek who had been around Brad and Diane during the months just prior to her death presented a completely different picture.

"I knew there was great tension in the marriage because Diane told me so," said Virginia Colvin, wife of the general manager at WUHQ-TV. "She told me there were money problems and that they were fighting a lot. It was obvious they weren't getting along."

She said it appeared Brad had been crying when the couple attended a WUHQ Christmas party in the middle of December.

Sahli also called to the stand the two cleaning women, Lori Osten and Carol Mendez. Although their testimony was brief, Sahli believed it was the final piece of testimony he needed to link Brad to the gun. He now had seven different people linking the weapon to Brad.

Sims attempted to discredit the women's testimony in cross-examination, but to no avail. They were independent witnesses with nothing to gain from testifying. In fact, they had reluctantly come forward because they had been forced to do so by an anonymous call to the Silent Observer line. It was obvious they didn't want to be there, and Sahli thought that helped his case.

While the cleaning women's testimony was important, everyone in the courtroom was anxiously anticipating the testimony of Julie Cook and Anne Hill.

The two women were a study in contrasts.

Julie Cook looked like the typical college student. Wearing blue jeans and a maroon sweatshirt, the long-haired brunette was open and friendly. She chatted with people in the hallway outside the courtroom before and after she testified. She didn't seem embarrassed at all about her relationship with Brad.

Anne Hill, on the other hand, was subdued. She entered the courthouse accompanied by a friend, refused to talk with reporters and immediately left the building after testifying.

She was also concerned about Court TV. She pleaded with the court not to allow her face to be shown during her testimony. She appeared nervous and embarrassed. Sindt granted her request, ordering the television cameras not to take her picture. However, he did allow

Court TV to continue to transmit the audio portion of her testimony to the nation.

When Cook finally took the witness stand, it was anticlimactic. Restricted by the court's rulings, Sahli gained little from her testimony. Her relationship with Brad was purely sexual, and if the judge wouldn't allow her to talk about that, there wasn't much else she had to say. She was only on the witness stand for 20 minutes. Sims didn't even cross-examine her. He didn't need to. He had effectively blunted her testimony in his previous arguments to the court.

Anne Hill was a different story. Her relationship with Brad went far beyond the quick afternoon trysts that had characterized Brad's relationship with Cook. Hill seemed to have genuinely liked Brad, and appeared to be angry over being used by him. She was the woman scorned.

During Hill's one hour on the witness stand, Sahli seemed to be walking on egg shells. He gingerly led her through his questioning, not wanting to violate any of Sindt's rulings. He needed her testimony, but he also didn't want to risk the possibility of a mistrial.

The nervous trek through dangerous territory was worth it for Sahli. Hill was a damaging witness to the defense. She seemed to be at the center of many issues Sahli had been focusing on throughout the trial.

Although Sahli couldn't question her about the sexual relationship she had with Brad, he didn't need to. She had enough damaging things to say about Brad without getting into the sexual aspect of their relationship. Besides, the jury would be able to make their own assumption after hearing her testimony about their teacher/pupil relationship.

She didn't look at Brad during the entire time she was on the witness stand.

The magnitude of her testimony could be seen in Brad's face. He wiped sweat from his brow continually as she told the jury how she had met him in the fall of 1990 while taking a criminology class at WMU. She said they had developed a friendship because they had a lot in common.

Hill, a divorced mother of two small children, said Brad had told her his wife had left him and that he was a single parent raising his child alone. She said he had led her to believe that his wife was in the process of divorcing him.

It was dangerous testimony, especially in light of what the jury already knew. They had heard extensive testimony about the night Diane had received the threatening letter on Halloween Eve. They also knew the dates of Diane's trips to Detroit to visit her parents.

On each of those dates, Sahli was able to tie Hill to Brad. She told the jury she had spent a couple of hours with Brad on Halloween Eve. She said that Brad had later told her Diane was upset because he was late returning home from WMU. He had also told her that Diane had been babysitting Marler for him, implying the couple was not living together.

The jury knew the truth. The reason Diane was mad was because she had been terrified by the threatening letter and had spent several hours at Cindy Accusta's house waiting for Brad to return home from WMU.

Hill also told the jury that Brad once had invited her to his Marshall home for the evening. The date was Dec. 19, the weekend Diane was in Detroit visiting her parents. The jury knew that, too.

She also testified that Brad tried to contact her on Feb. 8, the day before Diane was killed. He left a message on her answering machine indicating he wanted to "get together" with her that evening. The jury knew that Diane and the kids were in Detroit visiting relatives on that night.

When Hill returned his telephone call the next morning—the day Diane was murdered—Brad told her he couldn't meet with her that evening because he was "leaving town for the weekend," a fact the jury also knew wasn't true.

Hill also testified that on several occasions Brad seemed to be extremely upset with his wife over things Diane had said and done.

"He was especially angry because Diane had frozen his bank accounts and he could no longer pay for the classes he had signed up for that semester," Hill said. "He was angry because he couldn't take the graduate courses he wanted to take, and he felt that would interrupt his plan to get a doctorate degree."

That conversation, she said, occurred in late January, only a few days before Diane was killed.

"There's the motive," Diane's sister, Darlene, whispered to a friend seated next to her in the courtroom.

Hill had other damaging testimony. Again it was directly in line with what Sahli had wanted the jury to hear all along.

In late fall, after they first met, Brad was trying to impress Hill with stories about himself. He told her he was a firearms expert and a first-rate marksman.

"He told me he was an excellent shot with a rifle," she said, looking towards the jury. "He said he preferred hunting with a bow and arrow because there was no sport for him in hunting with a rifle. He said he could kill anything instantaneously because he was such a good shot."

Several members of Diane's family could be seen wiping tears from their eyes. The vision of Diane being stalked by Brad was again vivid in their minds.

Hill also talked about a time in early fall when Brad had mentioned getting stuck knee-deep in a creek behind his house while tracking a deer.

"We were laughing about the fact that he almost broke his leg when he got stuck in the mud," she said. "He told me he was surprised how soft and mushy it was."

Several jurors scribbled notes on their legal pads, remembering where the rifle was found after Diane was killed.

Sims tried to counter her testimony, but his efforts were fruitless. Her story fit perfectly with what Sahli had been saying all along. After 20 minutes of prodding and probing Hill's testimony, he returned to his seat knowing her testimony was devastating for his case.

The battles Sahli had fought with Sims for weeks about Hill's testimony had paid off. Sahli had accomplished what he wanted. Her testimony fit his case like a glove.

Sahli spent the next two days trying to gather additional testimony from witnesses on the marital problems Diane and Brad went through for months, but Sims was back to his old antics. He objected strenuously to several of the witnesses, including Diane's life-long friend, Regina Zapinski.

Outside the jury's presence, Zapinski told the court that Diane had told her only days before her death that she was considering divorce. Diane also told Zapinski she was afraid Brad had found a girlfriend at WMU.

"He doesn't find me attractive anymore," Zapinski said of Diane's comments to her.

While her testimony was devastating to Brad, it was also hearsay. Sims argued it was inadmissable because the statements came from Diane and she wasn't here for him to cross-examine her. Sindt agreed and refused to allow Zapinski to testify in front of the jury.

Sahli was upset, but he was confident he had presented enough evidence.

The only other setback occurred on the last day of the state's case when Sahli called David Minzey, a Michigan State Police detective, to the witness stand. Minzey was part of the original task force that had investigated the murder, and he had prepared a lengthy report on the circumstances surrounding Diane King's death.

As soon as Sahli called Minzey to the witness stand, Sims objected.

He said Minzey didn't have enough experience to qualify as an expert witness and his theories would be speculation at best.

Minzey was prepared to say that Diane had not been killed by a stalker but, more likely, by someone who knew her well. He was also prepared to say that the threatening letter was not from an obsessed fan, but also from someone who knew her. He believed the same person had not sent the letter and made the calls, but whoever had sent the letter knew of the telephone calls.

"I think it would be a great closing argument," Sims said sarcastically. "This witness is not an expert. His testimony will be exceedingly more prejudicial than probative, and I don't think it's relevant of anything."

Sahli argued that it was relevant and would be beneficial to the "trier of facts." Sahli said Minzey's testimony would be the same as allowing an accident reconstruction expert to testify.

Sindt agreed with Sims. "I think great caution has to be given when one likens Mr. Minzey's testimony to an accident reconstruction expert," Sindt said. "We are dealing with human behavior which is not subject to the same principles as an accident reconstruction expert . . . I am not going to allow it."

The other matter that was hanging over Sims' head was the expected testimony of Ricky McClain, whom Sims had described as the "singing jailbird." Sahli had made it clear during the first days of the trial that he fully intended to call McClain to the witness stand.

Sims was praying that he wouldn't. Although he thought he could counter in cross-examination anything that McClain might say, he just didn't want to put any more thoughts into the jurors' minds.

His worries were unfounded. Just before the state rested, Sahli announced that he was unable to locate McClain, who had fled the area.

It really wasn't unexpected. Sims had always thought McClain's ploy was a self-serving attempt by a petty crook to gain favor with the district attorney's office.

So finally, after 67 witnesses covering five weeks of jury selection and testimony, Sahli rested the state's case against Bradford King.

"The state will have no more witnesses at this time," Sahli said. "The state rests."

Sims immediately asked Sindt to issue a directed verdict of acquittal.

Outside the presence of the jury, Sims said the court must view the evidence "in a light most favorable to the defendant." He told the judge that the prosecutors did not prove premeditation—the key element in determining first degree murder—nor did they prove the gun found in the creek was the murder weapon. And even if it was the murder weapon, they hadn't linked it to Brad King, Sims argued.

Sahli countered by saying he clearly had presented evidence tying King to the gun, and that he also believed the evidence indicated the gun was the murder weapon. He implored Sindt not to take the case out of the jury's hands.

"Let them decide this case, it's their job now," he said.

Freida leaned her head forward and cried quietly.

As he had done so many times in the past, Sindt took a lengthy recess before returning to the courtroom to announce his decision.

The delay was the last thing Diane's family wanted. Although Sims' motion was a standard procedure in any criminal case, Sahli had not prepared Diane's family for it, and they were obviously rattled by Sims' arguments. They truly believed there was a possibility that Sindt would uphold Sims' motion. During the recess, Diane's entire family gathered in a room adjacent to the court-room and prayed.

"This just can't happen now, not after all we have been through," a startled Darlene Goins said as the family filed back into the courtroom to hear Sindt's rul-ing. "We've come too far for the judge to do this to us."

"Don't worry, it's not going to happen," one of Sahli's assistants said.

"Considering all the evidence, although it is circum-stantial, there is enough evidence to put this case before the jury," Sindt ruled.

Sims seemed to know that his motion would be denied, and he quickly moved forward with his own evidence. Where the state's case included 67 witnesses over four weeks, Sims called only seven witnesses, who testified less than 90 minutes total. As had been expected, Brad King was not one of them.

Sims never said publicly why Brad did not testify, but his co-counsel, Virginia Cairns, told Court TV that the trial had left Brad emotionally unable to withstand the rigors of a cross-examination.

"Bradford King has been in jail almost a year," Cairns said. "He is completely distraught."

Regardless of what Cairns was telling the media, no one familiar with the case ever expected Brad to testify. He had too much to lose by exposing himself to Sahli's cross-examination. It was clear that Sims had held true to his earlier belief: that the case was going to be won or lost on his ability to cross-examine the state's witnesses, not by calling his own witnesses who would provide a different spin to the case.

Sims called a receptionist who had worked at WUHQ, three WMU students who had helped Brad clean the farmhouse, and a couple of Brad and Diane's neighbors.

The only interesting aspect of the defense's case was the testimony of David Ripley. In a surprising but unimportant twist, Ripley testified that he had moved into a house adjacent to the Kings' farmhouse on Division Drive a few weeks ago. Ripley said he had made a startling discovery while rummaging through the attic: he found a .22 caliber Scoremaster rifle identical to the one found in the creek bed.

It was extremely frightening testimony to Diane's family and friends. Speculation spread throughout the courthouse that the defense had enough ballistic evidence to cast doubt on which weapon had been used in the killing, and, in turn, who had committed the murder. However, the defense's evidence didn't materialize and Sims rested his case.

During rebuttal testimony, Sahli called his ballistics expert, Robert Cilwa, who quickly and thoroughly smashed any question about the gun. Cilwa, who had testified earlier in the case about the gun found in the creek, told the jury he had examined the rifle found by Ripley and it was obvious from the testing that the gun could not have fired the bullets that killed Diane. He also said that the shell casings found in the loft and in the creek bed were not fired from Ripley's weapon. Sims did nothing to try and counter Cilwa's testimony during cross-examination.

Sahli happily rested his case moments later. He smiled for one of the few times during the trial as he turned and looked at Diane's family.

"It's almost over," Sahli said to the group.

"Thank God," Darlene responded as the family hugged each other in the aisles of the crowded courtroom.

CHAPTER 23

DIANE'S FAMILY, WAITING for the closing arguments to begin, was seated in the first and second rows where they had been every day for the past six weeks. Several family members held hands. It had been a long trial, and they were anxious for a final determination.

Freida, seated in the second row, was extremely nervous. She wanted Brad in prison for life, not only as punishment for the death of her daughter, but to ensure that her grandchildren would always be by her side.

She was so desperate to make sure that she would always have her grandchildren that she had a plan to whisk the children to an Indian reservation in Canada if Brad was found not guilty.

Before the closing arguments could start, the two attorneys spent several minutes answering questions from the jurors about their one-hour trip to the murder scene the day before.

The trip, at Sahli's request, allowed the jurors to see first-hand the farmhouse, barn and fields where Diane died almost two years before. Under strict supervision, the jury spent an hour in an organized procession around the property. Brad was not allowed to go. He stayed behind in the Calhoun County Jail.

And now, sitting erectly at the defense table, he calmly watched Sahli walk to the podium.

Sahli appeared confident and relaxed.

"Ladies and gentlemen of the jury," he started. "This case began in the summer of 1990 when Mrs. Diane King received some telephone calls at the television station where she worked. It continued when she found the threatening letter in her mailbox."

Sahli, as he had been throughout the trial, was subdued. He gave the jury a methodical summary of the evidence. He paced back and forth in front of them, using charts, graphs, and slides to illustrate his points.

Holding the threatening letter in his hands, he turned and faced the jury.

"Diane was terrified by this note that she found in her mailbox," he said. "This note was prepared by someone who knew about the telephone calls. This note was designed to cause terror in the life of Diane King. And it did."

He moved from the threatening note to Brad's actions as a husband and father. He repeatedly referred to him as "our single parent." He spent several minutes going over details of telephone records and testimony that clearly showed a pattern of deceit and deception on Brad's part.

While Sindt had prohibited him from presenting evidence about Brad's sexual affairs, the testimony from Anne Hill and Julie Cook gave Sahli the opportunity to discuss at length Brad's friendship with the women.

Sahli's inference was clear and Sims knew it. About 20 minutes into Sahli's closing argument, Sims leaped from his chair and objected to comments the prosecutor was making about "visits" Brad had with the women. Instead of arguing in front of the jury, Sindt ordered them from the courtroom.

"What's your objection?" Sindt asked Sims.

"In my opinion he has tripped over the line again in regards to the court's previous rulings," he said. "And I move for a mistrial. He has clearly violated the court's rulings."

Freida shook her head in disgust, while other family members were frantic. They anxiously waited for Sindt's ruling, again not knowing what to expect.

"Judge, I don't think I have violated the court's ruling in any way," Sahli said. "It's a closing argument and I don't believe I have mistated any of the evidence."

Sindt agreed.

"I will sustain the objection with regards to the word 'visit,' but I see no grounds for a mistrial," Sindt said. "I don't find there to have been a violation of the court's previous ruling. Let's bring the jury back in."

The objection didn't seem to slow Sahli at all. He continued to tell the jury about Anne Hill and her trip to the Marshall farmhouse while Diane and the kids were in Detroit.

"Here is our single parent again," Sahli repeated for emphasis, "entertaining one of his students while his wife and children are away."

He accused Brad of lying not only to Diane, but to the coeds at WMU.

He then moved to the night Diane had been killed.

"The defendant expected Diane to return alone," he said. "He didn't expect the children to be with her. You heard the testimony. Freida called and told him Diane was on her way home. Not Diane and her children, but Diane. The original plan was for Diane to leave the children in Detroit, and that's what Brad thought she was going to do."

Sahli talked about the security measures that Diane had implemented after receiving the threatening letter.

"Diane's life changed when she got that letter on Oct. 30," he said. "That note changed the life of Diane King, and I submit to you that what you have heard during this trial are the actions of a terrified person. A person who was in fact placed in terror by the receipt of this note. I submit to you that Diane King didn't change her plans on Feb. 9.

"Diane King saw her husband that night. And after seeing him, she then got out of her Jeep Wagoneer. That's when she was shot two times. Once in the chest at a downward angle—the fatal shot that went through her heart. And a second time in the vaginal area—a shot which traveled straight up her body. Ladies and gentleman, I submit to you that is not the shot of a stranger."

"Wait, wait, wait," Sims said, rising from his chair. "Wait just a minute."

Sindt didn't even ask the nature of Sims' objection. He simply instructed the jurors to leave the courtroom.

Sims argued that Sahli's comments were not based in fact. He argued there had been no evidence presented at the trial that would allow Sahli to say the second shot was fired by someone who knew Diane.

"Where did that come from?" Sims asked incredulously. "Once again I move for a mistrial. The cumulative error is extremely prejudicial. This last comment is extremely ridiculous."

Sahli shook his head in disgust.

"I don't think so, your honor," Sahli said, citing several legal cases to defend his statements. "A prosecutor can draw inferences from the testimony, and that's what I am doing."

"I am going to overrule the objection. You can respond to it in your closing argument, Mr. Sims," Sindt said. "Let's bring the jury back in."

Sims was upset. He shook his head as he walked back to the defense table.

"This is not the shot of a stranger," Sahli continued as the jurors nestled back into their seats. "This is not the shot of an obsessed fan. This is the shot of someone who was close to Diane King. It is a shot of someone who was enraged by Diane King. This is a revenge shot.

This was a shot fired by the defendant. There has been no testimony of any struggle, any robbery, any sexual assault. This shot was no accident.

"This is the shot of this man right here," Sahli said, pointing to Brad. "The defendant, ladies and gentleman, shot and killed his wife."

Loud sobs could be heard throughout the courtroom as Diane's family passed Kleenex to each other to wipe away tears that were streaming down their faces.

Sahli criticized Brad for what he hadn't done when he found his wife's body.

"He didn't attempt to help her," he said. "He is a police officer trained in emergency situations. What did he do? He went to the telephone to seek help.

"What about the children? If your children are in the car, you are going to want to get those children out of the car," Sahli said, pounding his hand on the podium for emphasis. "If your wife is laying on the ground, you are going to want to go to your wife. Did the defendant ask about his wife? Did he ask about his children? No. He stayed on the porch. Concerned husband? Concerned father? No. He knew the outcome, he knew what was wrong with her because he is the one who shot her."

Once again Freida could be heard crying as Sahli talked about Diane and her children.

Sahli then switched to the evidence about the rifle. He said the evidence was clear: Brad King owned the murder weapon that had been found in the creek—the weapon that had killed Diane King.

"He can tell Detective Schoder that he sold the gun in 1984," he said. "Do you believe it? Use your own judgement."

Sahli also talked about Brad's demeanor, calling his actions at the funeral inappropriate.

And after more than two hours of plodding through the massive evidence, Sahli ended his opening half of the closing argument. The other half would come after Sims' closing statement.

"Ladies and gentlemen I asked you to look at everything. Put it in its place," Sahli said. "When you do that, you will conclude the people have indeed proven beyond a reasonable doubt that the defendant Bradford J. King is guilty of murder in the first degree and is guilty of possession of a firearm.

"When you consider all the evidence in this case, I ask you to return a guilty verdict on all counts."

The courtroom collectively sighed as Sahli turned and walked back to his table. He had started out slowly, gradually building his case piece by piece. It was convincing. Many people in the courtroom nodded as Sahli asked the jury to convict Brad King.

Now it was Sims' turn. His style was in direct contrast to Sahli's. As he was throughout the trial, Sims was energized.

"Brad King is innocent, and I told you that a long time ago in a galaxy far, far away," he began. "There have been 89 different theories on how this murder could have occurred. But what are the facts?

"The fact is that Diane King died. I am sorry about that. I feel sorry for her family and I feel sorry for her husband. But that is a fact. Diane King is dead. It's a terrible thing, but she died."

Sims continued on strong. His attack, as it had been throughout the trial, was aimed at the sheriff department's investigation of the case.

He asked the jury to try to understand why, after almost a year, they decided to arrest Brad King.

"What evidence did they discover to change their minds?" Sims asked. "Why did they finally decide to charge him with murder? What was new? Nothing was new. Nothing changed. But why did they do it?"

Sims repeatedly pointed to the fact that no one could tie Brad King to Diane's murder. No one even testified that Brad King was at the scene when Diane King died, he said.

"There is a failure of evidence here," he said. "But the prosecutor wants you to make that giant leap of faith. They want you to convict a man of murder, but there's a problem. There is no evidence."

Brad listened quietly to Sims' statement. He showed no emotion. His mother, who was seated behind him, dabbed her wet eyes with a white kerchief.

"You want to know what it's all about, folks? That's what it's all about, right there," he said, pointing to the Court TV camera in the back of the courtroom.

"See it? It's the big production. The Calhoun County prosecutor's office, in conjunction with the Calhoun County Sheriff's Department, the Michigan State Police, the Michigan State Police crime lab, the FBI, and every other police agency in the whole county have put together the big production.

"When you don't have the proof, what do you do? You put together the big production. See the script? I've seen it. You've heard it. That's the script. We've got screenwriters. We've got lighting. We've got a big budget. We've got lasers, tazers, microwaves. We've got it all. It's a massive production. That's what it's all about. The big trial. And this dog and pony show, as I refer to it, is a circus act complete with its own magic. That's what we've got here, sound and fury signifying nothing."

Sims questioned why none of the neighbors had seen Diane King come onto the property that night. Several witnesses testified about not seeing any strangers in the area, but who saw Diane come home? he asked.

"Think about that."

He criticized Sahli for "nit-picking" Brad's statements to police. His wife had just been killed, he said. Sims questioned how anyone could know what was going on in Brad's mind at the time of the funeral.

"There was a big question of who did this and why.

Brad didn't know," he said. "His wife has been killed. He's confused. Yes, when a loved one dies, it's confusing. You heard the testimony, it was confusing for Freida and I accept that. It was confusing for Allen Marler and I accept that. Why can't they accept the fact that it was confusing for Brad King? Ask yourselves that. God forbid that some day at a funeral you don't act appropriately."

He also gave the jury several scenarios about what might have happened the night Diane died.

"I don't know what happened, but I don't have to know," Sims said. "I don't have to prove anything. He does. The burden of proof rests with the prosecutor, not with the defense."

Sims moved rapidly from one piece of evidence to another.

"I'm not going to tell you there was a stalker," he said. "I'm here to tell you one thing and one thing only. They haven't proved their case. And you know that. Those are the ideals you live by here. They didn't prove their case beyond a reasonable doubt. And you can't convict Brad King because you think he doesn't look right. You can't convict him because he didn't act right at his wife's funeral. You can't convict him because he is not a very nice person. You can't convict him because you don't like the way he sits or the way he moves. You can't think him into jail or guess him into a conviction. You have to know beyond a reasonable doubt that he is guilty. And they haven't proved that. They have a lot of good theories, but they haven't given you one theory that works."

He criticized the evidence about the gun.

"The major failing of this case is simple—the gun they found in the creek," he said. "Their own expert says he can't say positively this is the weapon that fired those bullets.

"And they want you to believe that Diane Newton

King would never have gotten out of that car unless her husband was right there. There is no proof of that."

He questioned how Sahli could claim Brad had designed a master plan to commit the murder.

"Bradford King is such a wonderful, whirlwind planner, and he knew that gun was out there on the 10th, why the heck not go get rid of it?" he said. "Great plan telling all these gals you're a single parent. Yeah, you're getting ready to off your wife and you're telling these people? How much more trouble could he have put himself in? Great plan."

He also criticized Freida's telephone call to Brad the night Diane was killed.

"The tragedy of this whole case is they don't like each other," he said of Brad and Freida. "If there hadn't been that animosity between them maybe we wouldn't be here today. Maybe things could have worked out."

He had been intense during the first stages of his closing statement, but now he was angry.

"The one thing that makes me madder than anything else in this case is that when Brad finds his wife, he calls for help," he said. "And the dispatcher tells him to stay on the line. He did what he was told. Then what happens. They say, 'Gee, he left his kids sitting in that car for 45 minutes.'

"Ladies and gentlemen," Sims said, his voice rising in anger, "how many police officers were at the scene? How many of them grabbed those kids and took them out of the car. You know the answer. Did anybody stop and think about those kids? Sure, their father did. He tried to get them out. But what did the police do, they ordered him to stay on the porch. And then they use it against him because he did what he was told."

Sims was genuinely angry. He stared at the jury.

"When the police arrived, they knew who committed this crime. They decided that night who did it and then they went out and tried to prove it. I swear to you, folks,

I think if Jack Schoder had seen some guy standing out in the middle of the street with a sign saying, 'I killed Diane King' with blood on his hands and a gun in his other hand, he'd have run him over trying to get to Brad King down there to sweat him a little bit. Cause he had already made up his mind."

He criticized the sheriff's department for failing to investigate the threatening letter when Diane had first received it.

"She went to them for help and what did they do? Nothing. No fingerprints, nothing. They didn't do anything until after she died. Then they decided to do something."

He stopped and searched his yellow legal pad for notes.

"I'm sorry folks, but they just didn't prove it," he said. "Despite all the media and all the hoopla, they didn't prove it. I don't know what happened and I am not going to try to make you believe something. Folks, I am not going to stretch. I'm not going to ask you to make that huge leap that they are asking you to do.

"Over a month ago when this dog and pony show began, I asked you to do something for me. Now I am demanding that when you go back there you do what the law and the evidence requires you to do. You send this man back to what's left of his family because they just didn't prove it, folks."

Sims turned away from the jury and made his way back to the defense table, where Brad King sat motionless.

The jury stared straight ahead. No one seemed pleased with Sims' statements, least of all Sahli, who now stood, ready to present the final part of his closing statement.

"Mr. Sims said there is one fact the people have proved, that Diane King has died," he said, his face turning a deep crimson. "I submit to you we have proved that Diane King was murdered.

"Mr. Sims says the people have given you 89 different theories about what happened. I submit to you the people have presented one theory: The defendant shot and killed his wife.

"Ladies and gentlemen, I asked you to decide this case based upon the facts, the evidence and the law. If you do that, I believe your verdict will find Bradford King guilty of murder in the first degree. Thank you."

Sahli stopped and took a deep breath. It was finally over. For two years he had lived with this case, but now it was done. It was out of his hands.

He walked back to his table as Sindt excused the jury, telling them to return at 8:30 A.M. the following day to begin deliberations.

Brad sat quietly, waiting to be taken back to the small holding cell adjacent to the courtroom. Sims leaned over and shook his hand.

Outside in the hallway, Freida and several members of Diane's family hugged Jack Schoder.

"They told me they were satisfied with how I handled the investigation, no matter what happens," he said, a wide smile creasing his face.

The jury had deliberated for over two days when the buzzer rang in Judge Sindt's first-floor office about 11 A.M. Monday. The news wasn't good.

"At this point, we are a hung jury and need further instruction," the note said.

Word spread fast through the courthouse. It was a dramatic surprise. The deliberations seemed to be going smoothly during the first two days. They had asked for the testimony of Deputy Guy Picketts, the first law enforcement officer on the scene. They had also listened to the direct testimony of Schoder. But there had been no indication that the jury was deadlocked.

No one knew what to think of the jury's note. Diane's family huddled in a witness room adjacent to the courtroom where they tried to console each other. They had horrified looks on their faces. They refused to allow themselves to think what might happen if the jury couldn't reach a verdict.

"I will not let myself even consider that possibility," said Diane's sister, Darlene, as she paced outside the small room. "It just can't, and I won't."

Sahli, smiling and confident after his closing arguments Wednesday, was ashen-faced when he entered the courthouse Monday shortly after the jury's announcement. He walked briskly to Sindt's chambers, refusing to answer reporters' questions.

Sims, on the other hand, didn't appear to be troubled. It was a good sign for him. Even though he didn't know what the vote count was, he knew he had at least one juror on his side. He smiled and shrugged his shoulders as he made his way through the crowd to Sindt's office.

Sindt decided to bring the jury back into the courtroom to see what was wrong. Although he was prohibited from asking what the vote count was, the judge seemed patient and not overly disturbed by the problem that had arisen.

The packed courtroom sat in stunned silence as the jurors solemnly walked to their seats. The look on many of the jurors' faces indicated the intense pressure they were feeling. One juror clutched a handkerchief, wiping tears from her eyes.

Sindt, in a calm, stern voice, told the jury to return to the jury room and resume its deliberations. He told them that they must all agree on the same verdict. He asked them to reconsider each other's position.

"As you deliberate, you should carefully and seriously consider the views of your fellow jurors," he said. "Talk things over in a spirit of fairness and frankness.

"Naturally, there will be difference of opinion. You should each not only express your opinion but also give the facts and the reasons on which you base it. By reasoning the matter out, jurors can often reach agreement."

Sindt ordered the jurors to rethink their own views and to change their opinion if they decided they were wrong.

"However, none of you should give up your honest beliefs about the weight or effect of the evidence only because of what your fellow jurors think or only for the sake of reaching agreement."

About 10 minutes after the jurors returned to their deliberations, Sindt passed a note to them asking what they wanted to do for lunch.

They decided they wanted to do what they had done in the past: recess for lunch. Sindt approved their request and ordered them to return to the courthouse at 1:15 P.M.

Their decision to break for lunch was viewed by many in the courthouse to be an indication that it was going to be a long deliberation.

Most of the jurors left by themselves, hurrying to their vehicles to escape the intensity of the small jury room.

The large crowd that was hanging around the halls of the courthouse nervously waiting for the jury's verdict didn't even have time to settle in after lunch when the buzzer again rang in Judge Sindt's office. It was 1:55 and word spread rapidly that they had reached a verdict.

The massive crowd of spectators quickly assembled in the courtroom. A few seconds later, a weary jury filed slowly into the courtroom. None of the jurors looked at Brad, instead staring at the floor or looking directly at Sindt.

"Have you reached a verdict?" he asked.

"Yes, we have," the jury foreman said. "We, the jury, find Bradford King guilty of count one, first-degree premeditated murder. And guilty of count two, possessing a firearm during the commission of a felony."

The reaction in the courtroom was subdued, primarily because Sindt had told the crowd he wouldn't tolerate any outbursts. Brad, who had remained seated at the defense table, sunk his bright red face in his hands. It was obvious he was floored by the jury's decision.

Diane's family began to hug each other and wipe tears from their eyes. Their reaction remained subdued until the judge and jury left the courtroom. Then they laughed and cried, hugged and kissed.

"Oh, my, I've waited so long for this," Freida said as she hugged Denise and Allen tightly. "It's over. It's over."

Sahli, as he had done so many times during the case, disappeared out a side door and declined to talk with reporters.

Sims was subdued. He told reporters there would be an appeal.

"There is error everywhere," he said. "I had 16 motions for a mistrial. Somebody will probably be doing this case again."

Jurors later said their original vote was six to six, but that during two days of intense deliberations, five jurors had changed their minds to guilty. That left one juror voting not guilty late Monday morning. That juror changed his mind after listening to Sindt's instructions to reconsider all of their positions.

During an interview with the *Battle Creek Enquirer*, juror Tamra Henriques said it was impossible for the jurors to ultimately believe that anyone else could be responsible for Diane's death.

"There were a lot of things that just didn't make sense for someone else to have done it," she said. "It just didn't add up."

Outside the courtroom, Diane's sister, Denise, spoke for the family.

"I am happy," she said as tears streamed down her face. "It's not going to bring my sister back, but at least we are not going to lose the children. Brad's selfishness took their mom and dad from them. Now they are going to spend the rest of their lives without parents.

"I wanted the man to pay, but I knew he was going to meet his maker someday. I was more concerned that if he did get off we would never see the children again. That's what we were worried about."

When asked what the family would tell Marler and Kateri, Denise began to sob.

"All I can tell them is that there is sin in this world and people do bad things," she sobbed as she clutched a large picture of Diane in her arms. "I am going to tell them that they have to forgive him. I am not going to let them grow up full of hate. That's not what Diane would have wanted for her children."

EPILOGUE

THE DAY FINALLY came for Diane King's family.

On a cold wintery morning in early January, Brad King was given the mandatory punishment for first degree, premeditated murder—life in prison.

Judge Sindt had no choice. It was the law.

Sahli did not speak. There was no need. Sims said only a few words.

Although Sims was respectful of Judge Sindt, it was apparent he was still angry and frustrated by the court's denial for a change of venue and the jury's guilty verdict.

"There is nothing that I can say that is going to change the sentence mandated by law," Sims said. "But I would say the outcome of this trial was in no uncertain manner impressed by the pressure presented to Mr. King and the community by the public opinion in this case. There was immense pressure in this matter for conviction.

"It's my own personal opinion that there was pressure by the media and by public opinion to the point where it was impossible to obtain a fair trial which would be uncolored by the media pressure and public opinion in regards to my client."

He acknowledged that, legally, the case was closed. But he went on to say that the intense pressure applied on

253

the jury by the community had created the insurmountable task for the defense to establish that somebody else did it. He said the pressure for conviction had shifted the burden of proof from the prosecution to the defense. Instead of being presumed innocent, he said, Brad King had been presumed guilty.

The only request he made was to allow Brad to serve his life sentence in a federal prison, instead of a Michigan state prison.

"Given my client's past experience as a police officer, I strongly urge you to place him in a federal prison to protect him from people who may have scores to settle with him."

That was it. Sims' work was completed. Although there was no doubt that Brad would appeal his conviction, it was clear Sims would not be handling the appeal. Brad did not have money to pay him. A court-appointed attorney would now take over his case.

Denise Verrier, Diane's sister, had been chosen to speak for the family. She could have been Diane's twin. She was beautiful, articulate and brave.

She walked slowly to the podium, clutching her speech in her hand. She began to cry even before a word had crossed her lips. Brad sat impassively nearby.

"We were all devastated by Diane's death and we miss her dearly," she began. "Diane was always so chipper and full of life. Every trip to Battle Creek, I half expect to see her walk through the door and hear her say, 'I'm here. Let's go to lunch.' We were not able to be at her side the night she died. It was all so confusing and unbelievable. She lay there all alone in the hospital by herself. Diane was devastated by the death of her father when she was 9 years old. And now, ironically, her children have suffered the very loss she hated so much. But her children have lost two parents.

"The death of her father affected her whole life and who she was. She was never really happy until she learned the gift of serving others. If there was a soup line nearby, Diane was there helping. She wanted her children to grow up with that same spirit of giving of themselves.

"Diane had so many plans for her children and how she wanted to raise them. She had put in an order for a baby lamb for Marler to raise. Mom had planned to give him some laying hens for his third birthday. Diane's mind was busy, at one time planning to fill the barn with life, a lifestyle she had had as a little girl with her own daddy. She wanted to be home with her children. Diane wanted to plant wildflowers down the lane where she could walk when showing everyone the deer on the property. She was so proud of that farm. She wanted to make it a home for her children.

"Diane was sensitive and compassionate. She was never late or one to forget your birthday. My phone will never ring on my birthday with Diane's voice wishing me a happy birthday. We will not be sending her a birthday card or calling her every year. Instead we will be visiting her grave. When we take the kids to the zoo, it won't be a fun day for Diane and the kids because Diane won't be there. A family reunion was planned by Diane. She looked forward to seeing some cousins and other relatives she has not seen in years.

"The reunion did not take place and Diane won't be able to be at the next one. I was not able to share the same mirror while putting on our makeup, the way we always used to do, for our brother's wedding. I'll never be able to see her face in the mirror again.

"Our lives have been affected in so many ways. I have nightmares of her struggling, trying to turn over to get to the car to protect her children. Only last night I dreamed that Diane did not die and she put my hand on her wounds. It was so real. If only it were real, she would be here for her children today.

"I am sure for the rest of my life I will look out the window every year on Feb. 9 at 6:15 or 6:30 and remember her and how alone she was out there on that cold gravel drive—all alone, with only her crying children to be heard. In light of the events that have taken place these past two years, I have asked why. When there was no arrest, why do the wicked go unpunished? Why do the innocent suffer so many times? One thing I came to realize was through all this there comes a time to stop asking why and start trusting. And that's what we did. I know this may sound simplistic, but I do feel this is really what God wants. We are people called to live by faith.

"I know that an impact statement is meant to make an impact on deciding the sentence of the defendant. In this case, by Michigan law, his sentence is mandatory life in prison—no parole. We are grateful for that. He should not win an appeal and be released because of a mere loophole."

When Denise finished, she walked back to her family where they embraced.

Brad wasn't moved by Denise's soliloquy. His statement to the court was mired in self-pity. If anyone expected Brad to confess, or even show the faintest hint of remorse, they were disappointed.

He was angry, defiant. He attacked the prosecutor, the judge and the jury. He didn't have anything to lose and he knew it. Even if it angered the judge, there was nothing Sindt could do to enhance the punishment. Brad knew going in what the sentence was to be.

As he had done so many times in the past, he blamed everyone but himself for his predicament. Where Denise's statement had been grief-stricken and sad, Brad's comments were angry and contemptuous.

"Presumed innocent. The basic tenet of the justice system. Presumed innocent did not exist in this case. The prosecutor's zealousness for the public's right to know obliterated the foundation of justice. What occurred throughout the investigation and the trial is a conspiracy to convict at any cost, otherwise known as vigilantism.

"The obvious victims of this farce are my wife, myself, our children, our families and our friends. The not-so-obvious victims are the citizens of this county and the justice system. My heart is saddened and angered at the loss of my wife and my freedom, and the effect this has had on our children, family and friends. For those who have to live with a corrupt justice system, I should have pity. I don't. You have the ability to change your justice system, and you deserve what you have until you change it. You may think this statement is harsh, but it explains my position."

Brad paused for a moment, shuffling his notes in his hands. He looked directly at Judge Sindt, focusing all his attention on him.

"First, you forced a trial in this county on me. You forced a jury on me, a jury with considerable prior knowledge of this case and obvious opinions. Second, you allowed the prosecutor, your friend, to continue to attempt to enter inadmissible testimony in this trial. Third, you remained the trial judge while you knew you were biased for the prosecution. Fourth, you knew that to ensure a conviction the only way was to cover up the incompetence of the investigation into the death of my wife. Fifth, this case carried a lot of media coverage and political impact. Control of the trial process was necessary in order to ensure a conviction. Why were these points carried on in this trial? To cover your guilt and the conspiracy to convict me. To cover your guilt and the travesty of justice you knew this to be.

"To the jury I charge you with failure to follow the court rules. I charge you with lying during the selection process. I charge you with willful misconduct. You also threw out the basic tenet of presumed innocent. I say you chose to act in the manner you did for your own comfort and not in the interest of justice. I have nothing but contempt for you.

"Finally, I stand here a proud man. I did not kill my wife. I am not guilty."

Compelling True Crime Thrillers
From Avon Books

THE BLUEGRASS CONSPIRACY
by Sally Denton

71441-8/ $5.50 US/ $6.50 Can

FREED TO KILL
by Gera-Lind Kolarik with Wayne Klatt

71546-5/ $5.50 US/ $6.50 Can

TIN FOR SALE
by John Manca and Vincent Cosgrove

71034-X/ $4.99 US/ $5.99 Can

"I AM CAIN"
by Gera-Lind Kolarik and Wayne Klatt

76624-8/ $4.99 US/ $5.99 Can

GOOMBATA:
THE IMPROBABLE RISE AND FALL OF
JOHN GOTTI AND HIS GANG
by John Cummings and Ernest Volkman

71487-6/ $5.99 US/ $6.99 Can

The Best in Biographies from Avon Books

IT'S ALWAYS SOMETHING
by Gilda Radner   71072-2/$5.95 US/$6.95 Can

RUSH!
by Michael Arkush
      77539-5/$4.99 US/$5.99 Can

STILL TALKING
by Joan Rivers   71992-4/$5.99 US/$6.99 Can

CARY GRANT: THE LONELY HEART
by Charles Higham and Roy Moseley
      71099-9/$5.99 US/$6.99 Can

I, TINA
by Tina Turner with Kurt Loder
      70097-2/$5.50 US/$6.50 Can

ONE MORE TIME
by Carol Burnett   70449-8/$4.95 US/$5.95 Can

PATTY HEARST: HER OWN STORY
by Patricia Campbell Hearst with Alvin Moscow
      70651-2/$5.99 US/$6.99 Can

SPIKE LEE
by Alex Patterson   76994-8/$4.99 US/$5.99 Can

Buy these books at your local bookstore or use this coupon for ordering:

Mail to: Avon Books, Dept BP, Box 767, Rte 2, Dresden, TN 38225   C
Please send me the book(s) I have checked above.
❏ My check or money order— no cash or CODs please— for $_____is enclosed
(please add $1.50 to cover postage and handling for each book ordered— Canadian residents
add 7% GST).
❏ Charge my VISA/MC Acct#_____Exp Date_____
Minimum credit card order is two books or $6.00 (please add postage and handling charge of
$1.50 per book — Canadian residents add 7% GST). For faster service, call
1-800-762-0779. Residents of Tennessee, please call 1-800-633-1607. Prices and numbers
are subject to change without notice. Please allow six to eight weeks for delivery.

Name_____
Address_____
City_____State/Zip_____
Telephone No._____   BIO 1093

COMPREHENSIVE, AUTHORITATIVE REFERENCE WORKS FROM AVON TRADE BOOKS

THE OXFORD AMERICAN DICTIONARY
Edited by Stuart Berg Flexner, Eugene Ehrlich and
Gordon Carruth   51052-9/$9.95 US/$12.95 Can

**THE CONCISE COLUMBIA DICTIONARY
OF QUOTATIONS**
Robert Andrews   70932-5/$9.95 US/$11.95 Can

**THE CONCISE COLUMBIA
ENCYCLOPEDIA**
Edited by Judith S. Levey and Agnes Greenhall
                                  63396-5/$14.95 US

**THE NEW COMPREHENSIVE AMERICAN
RHYMING DICTIONARY**
Sue Young   71392-6/$12.00 US/$15.00 Can

**KIND WORDS: A THESAURUS
OF EUPHEMISMS**
Judith S. Neaman and Carole G. Silver
                                  71247-4/$10.95 US/$12.95 Can

**THE WORLD ALMANAC GUIDE
TO GOOD WORD USAGE**
Edited by Martin Manser with Jeffrey McQuain
                                  71449-3/$8.95 US